IMAGES
of America

Pittsburgh's Orphans and Orphanages

Margaret "Tootsie" Schall was born in 1916 and was raised in the Odd Fellows Home for Orphans in Pittsburgh with two of her siblings from 1920 until 1933. An orphan by circumstance, she grew up amidst a multitude of children in an institutional setting from the time she was a toddler until her high school graduation because her widowed mother could not care for her. Her story is the memoir of many. (Courtesy of Joann Cantrell.)

On the Cover: The cover image shows the faculty, staff, and students outside of the Toner Institute (previously known as the Seraphic Home) in October 1915. The Toner Institute moved to this building in the Pittsburgh neighborhood of Brookline in 1914, operating under the auspices of the Seraphic Work of Charity and administered by the Capuchin Franciscan Friars and Sisters of Divine Providence. (Courtesy of the Archives of the Capuchin Franciscan Friars/Province of St. Augustine.)

IMAGES
of America

PITTSBURGH'S ORPHANS AND ORPHANAGES

Joann Cantrell and James Wudarczyk

ISBN 978-1-4671-0803-4

Published by Arcadia Publishing
Charleston, South Carolina

Printed in the United States of America

Library of Congress Control Number: 2022944502

For all general information, please contact Arcadia Publishing:
Telephone 843-853-2070
Fax 843-853-0044
E-mail sales@arcadiapublishing.com
For customer service and orders:
Toll-Free 1-888-313-2665

Visit us on the Internet at www.arcadiapublishing.com

In memory of Margaret Schall Belleno (grandmother of author Joann Cantrell), whose story of endurance was important to share, and to all of the orphans like her who persevered while longing for a home of their own

Contents

ACKNOWLEDGMENTS

The authors are grateful to the following individuals and organizations who contributed to this book by providing photographs and sharing their knowledge of Pittsburgh's orphanages:

Gary Rogers of the Oakmont Historical Society; the Pennsylvania Department of Carnegie Library; Fr. Joseph Melee; the Archives of the Sisters of Charity of Seton Hill; Megan L. McCue, Holy Family Institute; Emily Bitting and Concordia Lutheran Services; Three Rivers Youth Services; the Jewish Community Center of Greater Pittsburgh; the Jewish Association on Aging (JAA); Helen Wilson, Squirrel Hill Historical Society; Tracy Ferguson, Avonworth Historical Society; Sr. Linda Yankoski, CSFN, Holy Family Institute; Fr. John Petrikovic, OFM, Cap. Archives of St. Augustine Friary; Dan Simkins, Avonworth Historical Society; Episcopal Church Home Archives; Ron Gruca, Pressley Ridge; Shelia Talarico, Glade Run Lutheran Services; Eva Johnson; Tinsy Labrie; Joyce Griffin; Larry Peterson; Joanne Meade; Rebecca Kennedy McVicker; Ron Todd; Jim Sleigh; the family of Christine D'Alessandro; the Independent Order of Odd Fellows (IOOF); Rauh Jewish Archives at the Heinz History Center; Archives and Records of the Catholic Diocese of Pittsburgh; Stella Neely; the McKiernan family; and Jessie B. Ramey, PhD.

Author Joann Cantrell gives special acknowledgment and appreciation to her grandmother Margaret Schall Belleno for sharing her story that needed to be told, and to her great-aunt, Jane Schall, for keeping a scrapbook with images that documented and preserved their lives growing up in an orphanage. Their stories inspired the concept of this book.

Introduction

My interest in orphanages began with a photograph of my great-great-grandfather James Caldwell surrounded by four of his six living children (see page 127). The 1891 portrait captured a moment shortly after his wife, Jessie, died in childbirth, leaving him to solo parent while working in the Duquesne steel mill. An immigrant with no family nearby to help, James turned to an orphanage run by his church to care for his children. Over a century later, it struck me that these children were not orphans—they had a living father who had taken them to a studio near the orphanage in Allegheny City (now Pittsburgh's North Side) to ensure they had a family portrait. In fact, the Caldwell story represents the experience of many Pittsburgh families who used orphanages as a temporary measure to deal with a childcare emergency.

While the circumstances of working-class families in the Steel City reflected patterns across the United States, Pittsburgh was a particularly intense crucible, with multiple forces forging the setting for an urban childcare crisis. Industrialization changed the nature of work in the city, as well as the landscape itself: mills, factories, and mines killed and maimed workers, leaving families without breadwinners, and blackened the skies and water, sickening the people. Immigration and migration cut families off from social networks of support; from 1880 through 1930, between half to two-thirds of all Pittsburghers were foreign-born or children of immigrants. In the same period, migration from the Upper South more than doubled the African American population, who experienced searing racism and economic exclusion. Rapid urbanization drew people into the crowded city for jobs, exacerbating abysmal housing and sanitation. Under these conditions, families were often just one mill accident or tuberculosis case away from a childcare crisis.

Like the Caldwell children, most residents in 19th- and early-20th-century institutions were not actually orphans, or what were called "full orphans." Rather, they had one, or even two, living parents and were termed "half orphans." For example, 94 percent of the children in Pittsburgh's Home for Colored Children (HCC) had one or both parents living, similar to 88 percent of children in the United Presbyterian Orphans Home (UPOH). The death of a spouse was the key precipitating event leading to children's institutionalization. Other reasons included sickness, mental health crises, desertion, and unwed motherhood. Families often experienced overlapping crises, such as the loss of housing following the death of a spouse. Parents cobbled together other forms of childcare before turning to orphanages; most depended on help from family or friends, required older siblings, especially girls, to look after their brothers and sisters, or even left young children home alone. Institutional care appeared to be a last resort.

For parents experiencing a crisis at the turn of the last century, public support provided few options. The government offered almost no social safety net, with "outdoor relief" programs granting limited direct aid such as coal, food, or shoes. Public almshouses were widely regarded as dreadful places, though they did permit families to stay together, and were one of the few institutions that accepted Black children. In 1883, Pennsylvania's legislature passed the 60-day law, aimed at limiting the stay of children in almshouses to a period of two months. However, even years later, Progressive-era reformers accused institutions of breaking the law, suggesting that desperate parents continued to use the poorhouse to meet their most basic needs.

Most of the assistance available to poor families came from private charities, including over 80 child welfare organizations founded in Pittsburgh starting in the 1830s. Most were built by religious associations in a great wave from the 1880s through the 1910s in a national period of institution-building that included orphanages, homes for young working women, old-age homes, and hospitals. Institution founders labeled children as "delinquent," "defective," or "dependent" and created separate facilities, which were also racially segregated. The Home for Colored Children, founded by an interracial group of women in 1880, was one of the few organizations serving African American families until after 1900, when Black-led institutions expanded, responding to persistent racism. Middle- and working-class women did most of this child welfare work, often as volunteers through their religious bodies—Catholic, Jewish, and various Protestant denominations—serving as institution founders, operating managers, and fundraisers. Orphanages also had paid staff, sometimes including widows who sought employment where they could live with their children.

The daily experience of children varied across institutions, though there were some commonalities. Homes typically served 50–60 residents at a time, while some of the largest, such as the Catholic orphanages, housed over 100. Some orphanages required children to wear uniforms, though many did not, often relying on endless donations of handmade clothing from women's sewing circles. However, children were often easily identified as orphans through their haircuts: staff frequently shaved the boys' heads and cut girls' hair short to address pest problems. Children slept in sex-segregated dormitory-style rooms with many beds, ate together in a common dining room, and had few personal possessions. Food was generally adequate, though not abundant, and also highly dependent on donations. While some institutions hired teachers and held lessons during the day, others sent children to the local public schools. Orphanages hosted picnics, field trips, and holiday celebrations, but they were undoubtedly difficult places to live, especially for young people experiencing family trauma, as suggested by the chronic problem of children rebelling, setting fires, and running away.

Fortunately, most children resided in orphanages temporarily while their parents worked to reunite their families. Parents paid a monthly boarding fee and remained involved with their children while in the orphanages; they wrote letters, visited, brought treats, monitored their health, and sent clothing. While institution managers held much of the power, parents negotiated constantly for what was best for their family and their children's needs. For instance, most orphanages had age limits, generally not admitting children younger than two and requiring children older than 12 to go back to their families or into a formal indenture placement where they would work until they came of age. Parents frequently negotiated with managers to take younger children or to keep older children a little longer.

In short, orphanages attempted to fulfill the temporary needs of working parents experiencing a childcare crisis, often the consequence of the social and economic conditions wrought by industrial wage capitalism. While the privately managed institutions could never fully provide for the child welfare of Pittsburgh families, many parents, like James Caldwell, used orphanages strategically to meet their own family needs, regain stability, and reunite with their children. The photographs collected in this volume provide crucial glimpses into the stories of those children, parents, families, and staff members during the era of Pittsburgh's orphanages.

—Jessie B. Ramey, PhD

Dr. Ramey is the founding director of the Women's Institute and associate professor of Women's and Gender Studies at Chatham University. She is the author of the award-winning book *Child Care in Black and White: Working Parents and the History of Orphanages* (University of Illinois Press, 2012). Visit jessiebramey.com for more information.

One

Concordia Orphans Home

Life for the average family in the 1880s was difficult for most and harsh for many. Meager wages for jobs offered no benefits, and dangerous work conditions took a toll. Medical care and vaccines were still years from being available, and the challenge of how to care for children was cause for concern.

When one parent died prematurely, the surviving mother or father was hard-pressed to feed, clothe, and educate their children, and for many, it was a desperate, losing struggle.

Parents and relatives turned to their local churches for assistance, including the German Evangelical Lutheran churches in Pittsburgh.

The care for orphans was considered mission work by churches. A parent or guardian was required to sign an official orphanage agreement wherein the child would be "relinquished to the sole and entire control" of the home. Children had to be at least two years old when entering the orphanage and were released at age 18. A parent could reclaim a child if circumstances improved and a stable Christian home could be provided.

On July 23, 1883, the Concordia Home was dedicated, and it welcomed its first children the next day. Unlike many orphanages of the time, the home on the farm was always able to provide food for the children residents, but the expectation was for each child to pitch in and work, completing daily chores that were assigned. Older girls worked in the kitchen or laundry and helped with childcare for the youngest orphans. Boys were responsible for taking care of the farm animals, milking cows, helping with the harvest, and doing other labor-intensive chores.

The number of children in the orphanage would fluctuate over the years. Five children entered in 1883, but only one year later, in 1884, the home had 44 children. Enrollment peaked in the 1920s at 76, but as society changed, it dropped in 1941, with only 27 children. By the time the doors closed and the last orphans were placed in private homes in 1958, Concordia had cared for more than 1,000 children.

As early as 1878, Rev. Frederick Wilhelm established Concordia's Evangelical Lutheran Concordia Orphans Home. Parish member Christian G. Oertel and his wife, Margaretha, lived near the Marwood station on a 46-acre farm. Since the couple had no children of their own, Reverend Wilhelm suggested the property would make a wonderful legacy, and upon Christian's death, the deed was released to provide a farm home for orphaned children. (Courtesy of Concordia Lutheran Ministries.)

A new building was constructed to house the children while Margaretha Oertel would continue to live in the original homestead. As soon as the building was complete and dedicated on July 23, 1883, plans began to provide a school for the first five children who entered the home. Initially, classes were held in a small room, but they were later moved to the second story of another building that was added. (Courtesy of Concordia Lutheran Ministries.)

By the end of 1884, there were almost 50 children in the home, and five years later, a second building was complete. The two-story, T-shaped building had an entire first floor with a dining room and kitchen. The second story was divided into a store room and a bedroom for boys. The original building was made into a bedroom for the girls. (Courtesy of Concordia Lutheran Ministries.)

The first building of Concordia Home was dedicated in 1883. The home was situated on a working farm that helped immensely to provide much of the food necessary for the children. In the early days, the remote location of the home proved challenging, as it was a tedious journey by horse and buggy and an even longer train ride that involved a mile walk from the station. (Courtesy of Concordia Lutheran Ministries.)

Financial support was crucial to the survival of the Concordia Orphans Home. A large donation was made by Gerhardt E. Niemann, who made his will in 1882, before the home was established. Niemann directed that his estate would be given to Concordia and bequeathed to erect an orphan asylum of the Evangelical Lutheran Church. His estate was worth $169,636, a tremendous amount in 1910. (Courtesy of Concordia Lutheran Ministries.)

Life on the farm was disciplined. Older boys often woke at 4:30 a.m. and fired the stoves to warm the buildings in time for the 6:30 rising bell. Animals had to be fed before breakfast was served at 7:00 a.m. The daily routine included morning chores, school, and more barn work for the boys and housework for the girls. (Courtesy of Concordia Lutheran Ministries.)

School curriculum mirrored the public schools with the addition of Bible classes and Lutheran catechism. All of the orphans attended school until the eighth grade. Boys who were good students were permitted to attend high school, but girls were not encouraged to advance their education. Many young females found work as maids or domestic workers in private homes. (Courtesy of Concordia Lutheran Ministries.)

The Concordia Ladies' Aid Society was formed in 1915 to give aid to the orphans' home to promote interchurch sociability among Lutherans. Generous donations were received from the community and local parishes that included fruits, vegetables, bread, clothing, material, linens,

and other goods. Some members of the group are in this photograph with orphans who are wearing clothing that was made by the Ladies' Aid Society. (Courtesy of Concordia Lutheran Ministries.)

Conrad and Louisa Weil were recent immigrants from Germany when they got married and settled in Pittsburgh in 1885. As a young mother, Louisa passed away from typhoid fever in 1898, leaving five children from the ages of one to 11 years old. A month after her death, Conrad placed the four oldest children—Karl, George, Marie, and young Conrad—under the care of Concordia Orphans Home. (Courtesy of the George Weil collection, privately held by Eva Johnson.)

A young George Weil stands beside his friend August Potrafke, both 15-year-olds, on the farm grounds of the Concordia Orphans Home in 1904. Weil would spend seven years there, and when he was 17 years old, he left the home, took the train to Chicago, and enrolled at Addison Teacher's Seminary in Addison, Illinois. (Courtesy of Eva Johnson.)

A schoolhouse for the Concordia orphans was erected in 1884, and Henry W. Lensner became the first teacher and housefather. In excerpts from his journals, Lensner gave detailed accounts that life was not easy being in charge of orphans. High standards were kept for behavior, class work, and chores; however, the children would often get into mischief and cause great worry and stress for Lensner, pictured here with a group in 1919. (Courtesy of Eva Johnson.)

This is a photograph of Henry W. Lensner and his wife, Louisa. Lensner was the headmaster of Concordia Orphans Home in Marwood, Pennsylvania, from 1897 to 1915. Though he had the reputation of being a stern, German Lutheran elder, journal entries conveyed the deep concern and sense of responsibility he had for the orphaned children under his care. (Courtesy of Eva Johnson.)

A group of young men at Concordia in 1906 includes George Weil at age 16 sitting in the center. Weil was rarely mentioned in the housefather's journals, except for two occasions. In July 1899, the housefather noted that George fell from the loft in the barn where the children were not allowed and suffered a concussion. Two years later, Weil ate some mushrooms and became sick but recovered from that also. (Courtesy of Eva Johnson.)

Shortly before leaving the orphanage at 17 years old, George Weil is pictured with classmates who grew from young boys together to become men. Weil was very studious and thrived under the mentorship of the headmaster, Henry W. Lensner. He graduated from the Addison Teacher's Seminary in 1912 and found a teaching position at the school of the Lutheran Church, Missouri Synod, in Sedalia, Missouri. (Courtesy of Eva Johnson.)

The Weil siblings George, Marie, and younger Conrad are pictured here in 1908. When they came to the orphanage in 1898, their father, Conrad Sr., agreed to pay $12 per month to house his children while he worked as a laborer in Pittsburgh. In 1910, he moved closer to the orphanage to work in a coal mine. There was occasional contact with his children through the years, but the father lost touch over time. (Courtesy of Eva Johnson.)

This photograph of Henry W. Lensner was taken in April 1941. Lensner served as headmaster of Concordia Orphans Home from 1897 to 1915. He passed away in 1952. (Courtesy of Eva Johnson.)

A real-photo postcard from 1910 shows the store of A. Krause & Son in Marwood, later to become Cabot, Pennsylvania. This store was at the Marwood train stop, where travelers from Pittsburgh would come to visit children at the Concordia Orphans Home. Getting to the orphanage involved a difficult mile-long walk from the store over a road often clogged with snow in the winter or mud in the springtime. (Courtesy of Eva Johnson.)

By 1958, it was deemed "a foregone conclusion" that no more children would be entering the Concordia Orphans Home due to overwhelming costs for care and upkeep of the farm. A social worker was hired to place the children in private homes, and the final group of orphans was placed by the end of the year, when Concordia ceased to provide care for orphaned children. (Courtesy of Concordia Lutheran Ministries.)

Two

The Odd Fellows Home for Orphans

In the early 1900s, the Independent Order of Odd Fellows was one of the largest fraternal orders in the United States with 1,200 lodges throughout the state of Pennsylvania. Membership in the organization was non-discriminatory and was made up of miners, ironworkers, and laborers. A basic requirement was to believe in the teachings of the Bible, especially the stories depicting strong morals, good friendship, and loyalty.

As a benevolent men's organization, members were committed to a strong belief in a principal mission of providing assistance to the widows of members and ensuring the upbringing of their orphans. By the early 1920s, a boom in the construction and establishment of statewide orphanages took place. Seen as a type of life and health insurance of the time, members could count on the Odd Fellows to care for them or their families if misfortune should arise.

The original Odd Fellows Home for Widows and Orphans was a 14-room frame Victorian house located on a two-and-a-half-acre lot in the Ben Avon borough in Allegheny County, Pittsburgh, along the Ohio River. Known as the Clendenning Homestead, the property was bought by Henry Sutmeyer, a member of the Pittsburgh Odd Fellows, and the deed was turned over to the organization in February 1891. The first home had 20 children and one widow living in it.

Within a decade, it was evident that more room was needed to house the growing number of orphans who had no one to care for them. In 1923, a much larger facility was built several miles closer to the city in the area known as Brighton Heights offering accommodations for 242 orphans. It was considered a state-of-the-art facility, complete with boarding accommodations, a dining hall, school, playground, barbershop, dentist office, and infirmary.

Census records show that thousands of orphans were housed in Pittsburgh, and the Odd Fellows made good on their promise to nurture and provide education. As society changed after World War II, so did the need for orphanages, and the Pittsburgh Home for Orphans eventually closed.

The Odd Fellows of Pennsylvania needed a home to care for deceased members' widows and orphans, particularly those with limited funds. It was a dream fulfilled when Henry Sutmeyer and his wife, Elizabeth, presented the organization with the deed to the Clendenning Homestead and property in 1891. Both images show children standing outside of the original Home for Widows and Orphans of Odd Fellows, located at 6627 Brighton Road in the community of Ben Avon, six miles northwest of Pittsburgh along the Ohio River. The orphanage was operated by the Independent Order of Odd Fellows (IOOF) at this location from 1891 to 1924. The Home for Widows and Orphans was sold in 1924 and was subsequently known as the Knights of Pythias Orphans' Home until 1931. (Both, courtesy of Avonworth Historical Society.)

The original Odd Fellows Home in Ben Avon was a Victorian house where one widow and 20 children lived, along with a matron who also taught school lessons. Many of the orphans were toddlers living together with school-aged children, as seen in this photograph from the late 1800s with images of the Odd Fellow officers inserted above. (Courtesy of Avonworth Historical Society.)

In 1923, a new building was constructed on Fleming Avenue by the Odd Fellows. The three-story, redbrick Colonial home in the Brighton Heights neighborhood offered accommodations for 242 orphans. It was considered a state-of-the-art facility, complete with boarding accommodations, a dining hall, school, playground, barbershop, dentist office, and infirmary to isolate children when they were ill. (Courtesy of IOOF.)

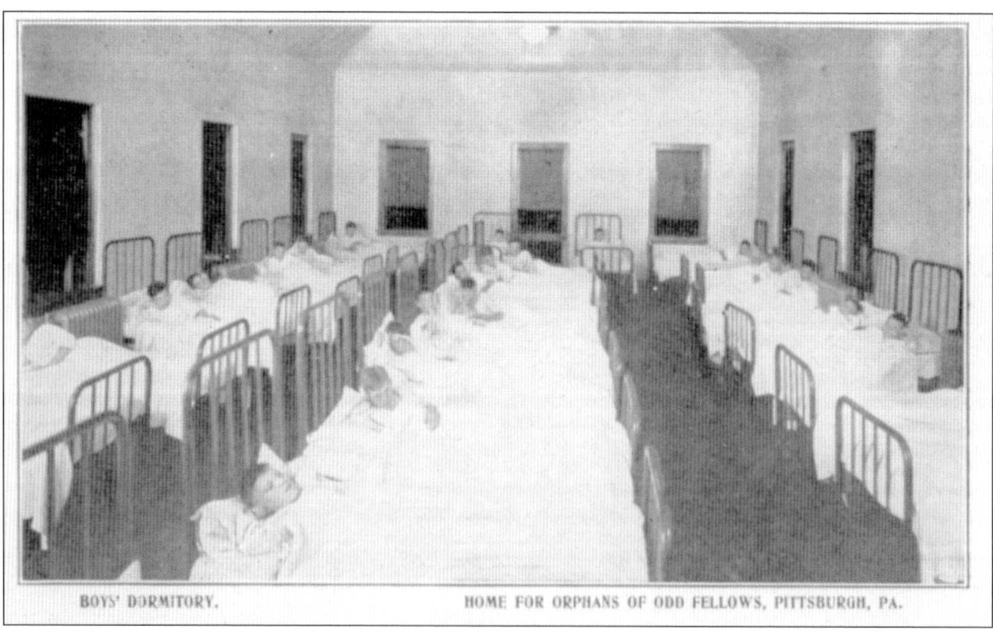

For the children at the Odd Fellows Home, everything was communal, and privacy was nonexistent. Young boys and girls slept side by side in an overcrowded dormitory, waited in long lines to use the lavatory, and shared everything with the other orphans they lived with. (Courtesy of IOOF.)

Orphans lost their individuality with a uniform appearance that is apparent in a photograph of the children gathering for a meal in the dining hall at the Odd Fellows Home. With identical haircuts and clothing, it is difficult to identify individual orphans in a group because they all looked alike. (Courtesy of IOOF.)

Boys and girls who lived at the orphanage had opportunities to learn a variety of skills and trades and develop hobbies and interests. Girls learned to sew, while boys were trained in woodworking, metalworking, and electrical work. (Courtesy of IOOF.)

A SECTION OF THE PLAYGROUND EQUIPMENT. HOME FOR ORPHANS OF ODD FELLOWS, PITTSBURGH, PA.

Pittsburgh philanthropists, donors, and businesses were generous in supporting the local orphanages with funding for special purchases like playground equipment for the children. Musical instruments were provided to encourage interest in the arts, and music lessons were offered, giving orphans the opportunity to join the orchestra or choir. (Both, courtesy of IOOF.)

"CHRISTIAN ENDEAVOR"—Sunday Afternoons—Come, visit. HOME FOR ORPHANS OF ODD FELLOWS, Pittsburgh, Pa.

THE CADETS—Home for Orphans of Odd Fellows, Pittsburgh, Pa.
Captain ARCHIE J. HOLMAN, Instructor

The Odd Fellows Home, as well as other orphanages, offered extracurricular activities for the orphan children to participate in, such as the athletic teams known as Cadets. The Cadets were a type of marching corps with flag drills and gave members a type of discipline while providing recreation. Cadets enjoyed friendly competition with other schools and often participated in regional championships. (Both, courtesy of IOOF.)

Children raised in the Odd Fellows orphanage were affectionately known to each other as "home kids" and became closer than siblings after living in tight communal quarters together for their entire childhood and high school years. The common bonds formed from shared experiences instilled empathy and understanding among orphans and often created a camaraderie that never weakened. As a testimony to the Odd Fellows' teaching and spirit of goodwill, friendships made in the orphanage lasted a lifetime, and extra effort was made to keep track of one another and stay in touch even through adulthood. (Both, courtesy of the Schall family.)

Young girls formed close friendships and created their own fun while living at the orphanage. Just as other young children would play in a schoolyard at recess, those who lived at the Odd Fellows would spend time outdoors on the grounds of the orphanage. The creative and playful spirit of teenagers trying to entertain themselves in the 1930s can be seen in these images. Girls would put on shows, make up skits, and pretend to be vaudeville performers, often improvising with costumes and hats that they had made themselves. (Both, courtesy of the Schall family.)

The 1920s through the 1930s were a period when few options existed to care for children who were abandoned or whose parents were unable to care for them. Orphanages like the Odd Fellows Home housed generations of children who lost one or both parents either to death, illness, or despair. The girls seen in these photographs entered the orphanage as toddlers and grew to become young women during the time that they lived there, hoping that circumstances would improve when they graduated and went out into the world as adults. (Both, courtesy of the Schall family.)

Census records show that in the early 1900s, orphanages in the United States housed more than 100,000 children, with thousands of those living in Pittsburgh. Children quickly learned that a benefit to being a home kid was the common bonds formed from shared circumstances. Empathy and understanding for those in the same situation created a lifelong camaraderie that never weakened. (Courtesy of the Schall family.)

As society changed after World War II, so did the need for orphanages, and the Odd Fellows Home eventually closed. Now part of the Pittsburgh Public School District, the original building still stands today, looking nearly the same as the original construction that housed hundreds of orphans for decades. (Courtesy of the Schall family.)

The photograph at left shows young Charles "Chuck" and Ruth Kress, who became the superintendents of the Odd Fellows Home in the 1950s. They made a vocation of treating forsaken orphans as if they were family and cared for them as grandchildren. During the holidays, when business owners would provide gifts for the orphans, the Kresses would secretly request items that each child needed, down to the exact sizes of shoes and clothing, or a toy of specific interest to make the children feel special. As they grew in age, the beloved couple made a lasting impression on hundreds of orphans they took under their wings, helping to put the love of God in their lives and offering the only semblance of a family that many orphans would ever know. (Left, courtesy of Stella Neely; below, courtesy of Rebecca Kennedy McVicker.)

Three

The Toner Institute

The Toner Institute, named for Dr. James L. Toner of Westmoreland County, Pennsylvania, was established in 1899 after the doctor's will provided a $140,000 fund to set up an orphanage for homeless boys. Originally housed at St. Joseph's Protectory, the orphanage became a Catholic industrial school administered by the Capuchin Franciscan Friars.

Twenty boys ranging in age from eight to 16 were transferred from St. Joseph's to the Toner Farm. There, the boys received an education, worked in the fields, and were taught various trades. Barns and other buildings were erected to house farm animals and equipment. The boys of the orphanage worked to cultivate the fields and provide fresh vegetables and dairy products. Any surplus was sold to local merchants or markets in the city so that the profits could help provide funding for the continued growth of Toner.

The Toner Farm was moved to the Pittsburgh neighborhood of Brookline in 1914 under the auspices of the Seraphic Work of Charity and administered by the Capuchin Franciscan Friars and Sisters of Divine Providence. The new superintendent assigned by the bishop was Rev. Sigmund Cratz.

Toner continued to thrive, and in 1927, a milestone in growth took place when the cornerstone was laid for the chapel Our Lady of Angels, completed and dedicated on September 14, 1930. Construction continued as more dormitories were added with recreation rooms, administration buildings, an infirmary, and a reception center. After World War II, the institute adopted the tone of a military academy, and the students were taught the fundamentals of military drill and discipline.

By the 1970s, the Toner Institute underwent major changes. Military uniforms were replaced, and the marching unit folded. The student population, down to just 47 boys, was no longer all Catholic, and the focus shifted to a home for boys with emotional problems. A cash crisis reached its peak in 1977, when the cost of providing for each student was more than $55 per student and fundraising campaigns were insufficient. On April 5, 1977, the board of directors announced their decision to close the institution as it had become obsolete.

Fifty acres of rolling land were acquired on a hilltop overlooking Brookline's Dorchester Avenue, stretching from Castlegate to Queensboro Avenues to the north, and bordering McNeilly Road to the south, to build a campus to house the orphanage. After many years of hard work and dedication, the campus began to take shape. (Courtesy of the Archives of the Capuchin Franciscan Friars/ Province of St. Augustine.)

The institution was officially chartered and the name was changed to Toner Institute and Seraphic Home. The building was located in a remote corner across the border in the neighboring community of Mount Lebanon, but the local newspaper, citizens, and municipalities continued to refer to the institution as being located in Brookline, even assigning an incorrect address and zip code. This geographical misprint continued throughout the Toner Institute's existence. (Courtesy of the Archives of the Capuchin Franciscan Friars/Province of St. Augustine.)

To aid with the construction of the administration building, which also served as a dormitory, school, and chapel, fundraising efforts were conducted by the Knights of St. George, the Ladies Auxiliary of the Seraphic Work of Charity, the German Catholic Society and Women's League, and the St. Vincent DePaul Society. Popular among these fundraising bazaars were Donation Day and Flower Day, events that were well attended, bringing in generous monetary donations. (Courtesy of the Archives of the Capuchin Franciscan Friars/Province of St. Augustine.)

The Faculty, Help and Pupils of the Seraphic Home, October 1915

Faculty, staff, and students pose for a group photograph outside of the Toner Institute (previously known as the Seraphic Home) in October 1915. The Toner Institute had moved to this building in the Pittsburgh neighborhood of Brookline a year earlier. Due to the hard work of the instructors and administrators and the generosity of donors, the Toner Institute was proud to announce in 1916 that 548 boys had received training and education since the school's opening. (Courtesy of the Archives of the Capuchin Franciscan Friars/Province of St. Augustine.)

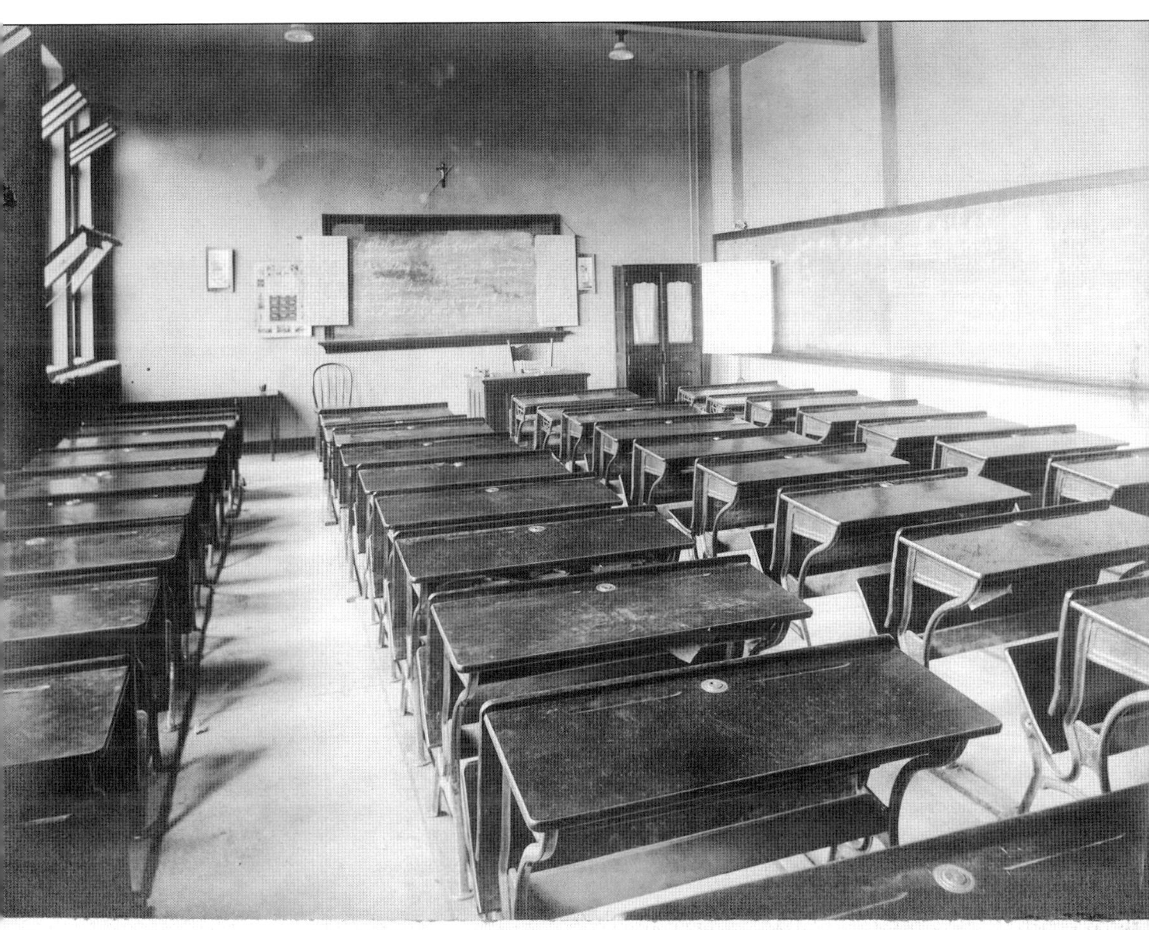
The Junior School Room on the North side of the Main Building.

This early photograph shows the inside of a classroom at the Toner Institute. (Courtesy of the Archives of the Capuchin Franciscan Friars/Province of St. Augustine.)

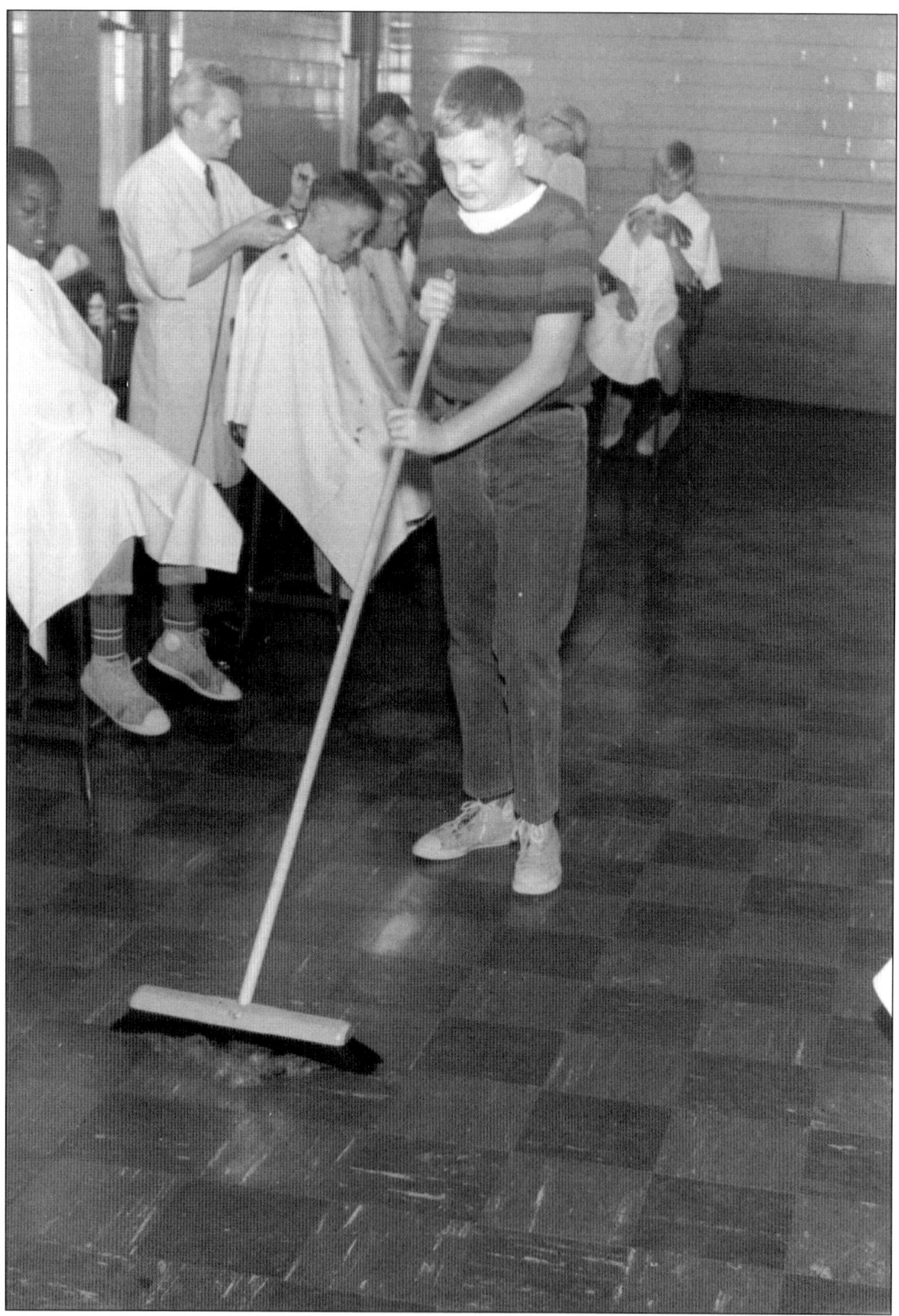

A young Toner student learns about work ethic and responsibility while on the job at the barbershop. (Courtesy of the Archives of the Capuchin Franciscan Friars/Province of St. Augustine.)

Throughout the years, the Toner students were often treated to visits from sports celebrities, such as Pittsburgh Pirate Manny Sanguillén, seen here at the school in the early 1970s. A fan favorite, he was a catcher for the Pirates when they won five National League Eastern Division titles between 1970 and 1975 and the World Series in 1971 and 1979. Sanguillén is pictured with the students and Fr. Kevin Miller, superintendent of Toner at the time. (Courtesy of the Archives of the Capuchin Franciscan Friars/Province of St. Augustine.)

An expansive campus included modern classrooms, a theater, gymnasium, auditorium, and library. Toner had grown and prospered, along with the thousands of students who were enrolled there and benefited from the institution's education and guidance during their formative years. (Courtesy of the Archives of the Capuchin Franciscan Friars/Province of St. Augustine.)

This aerial view from 1939 shows the Toner Institute's 50 acres on the hilltop campus. The student population numbered 130 children of grade-school age with 15 sisters in charge of teaching. By that period, there had been more than 5,000 boys trained at the Toner Institution. Although outsiders mistakenly considered Toner to be a secluded monastery, the community was encouraged to visit and learn about the boys and their daily activities. (Courtesy of the Archives of the Capuchin Franciscan Friars/Province of St. Augustine.)

Four

Caring for Orphans

In the early 1900s, orphanages in the United States housed more than 100,000 children, with thousands of those living in Pittsburgh. Buildings that became group homes were constructed through churches and fraternal organizations. The facilities, complete with boarding accommodations, dining halls, schools, playgrounds, and infirmaries, offered accommodations for 100 to up to 300 orphans at any given time. Parents faced hardships during rough economic times. Some widowers were immigrant laborers who placed their children in orphanages because they had to continue to make ends meet, and others were Civil War widows ill-equipped to be single mothers, left with no alternative but to turn their children over to institutional care. A brief list of orphanages established in Pittsburgh by some of the various groups and denominations include:

The Protestant Home, established in 1832 by the First Presbyterian Church, was the first agency for abandoned, neglected, and orphaned children west of the Allegheny Mountains. The second orphanage, known as the Home for the Friendless, was incorporated in 1861 by the Second Presbyterian Church. For the next 100 years, both institutions continued to serve the orphan population of children within the community on the North Side of Pittsburgh.

The Episcopal Church Home was chartered in 1859 as an asylum for aged and infirmed members of the Protestant Episcopal Church in Allegheny County. Now a senior community, the building has occupied the same spot at Fortieth Street and Penn Avenue since 1861, and during the Civil War, it opened its doors to war orphans.

The organization known today as Three Rivers Youth traces its origins to 1880, when local minister Rev. James Fulton could not find an orphanage to provide care and shelter for a four-year-old African American girl he found wandering the streets of Pittsburgh's North Side. Established by the efforts of activist Julia Blair and the Women's Christian Association, the Home for Colored Children became an unprecedented safe haven for children who were barred from all-white orphanages. The organization later became the Termon Avenue Home for Children. Three Rivers Youth was the result of a merger between the Termon Avenue Home for Children and a child welfare service agency called the Girls Service Club, founded in 1924 and incorporated in 1932 as a home for wayward girls. The two organizations merged to become Three Rivers Youth in 1970, and it is still in operation today serving the Pittsburgh community.

In 1891, Esther DeWolf Gusky founded the Jacob M. Gusky Hebrew Home and Orphanage in memory of her husband, a wealthy department store owner who was fond of children and had a passion for providing food and toys to orphans and those who were poor throughout the city.

These homes are only a few of the numerous institutions that provided for Pittsburgh's orphans and children in need in the late 1800s throughout the mid-1900s.

William Alfred Passavant, born in 1821 in Zelienople, Pennsylvania, was a Lutheran clergyman who dedicated his life to the establishment of charitable groups and the founding of numerous missions, hospitals, colleges, and orphanages. In 1854, he responded to a need and established the Orphan's Home and Farm School in the rural community of Zelienople, Butler County. Today, known as Glade Run Lutheran Services, the organization continues to operate with a tradition of compassion for children and families. William Passavant's legacy of caring continues on the 331-acre Zelienople campus, in dozens of public schools, through seven community offices, and in homes and communities throughout Western Pennsylvania. (Courtesy of Glade Run Lutheran Services.)

In 1854, the cornerstone was laid for the main building of the Orphan's Home and Farm School in Zelienople on the grounds of 25 acres purchased by founder William Passavant. The first eight boys were accepted into the home, and Rev. Gottlieb Bassler was named the first director. In 1862, the original main building was destroyed by fire. (Courtesy of Glade Run Lutheran Services.)

By 1860, the Orphan's Home and Farm School served 57 children ranging from five to 20 years old. An additional 375 acres were deeded from the Passavant family to the orphanage and farm. (Courtesy of Glade Run Lutheran Services.)

The children who lived at the Orphan's Home and Farm School learned to do chores from a young age, and performing the daily rituals of life on the farm were expected. In these images from the 1920s to 1930s, boys are pictured on a horse and feeding the chickens on the farm property. Such chores evolved through the decades but remained a part of daily life for the orphans until 1972, when the farm operations discontinued. (Both, courtesy of Glade Run Lutheran Services.)

In 1955, the name of the orphan's home was changed to become the Lutheran Children's Home of Zelienople. Children are seen packed into a car belonging to the organization with a driver who would provide transportation when the orphans had outings in the community. (Courtesy of Glade Run Lutheran Services.)

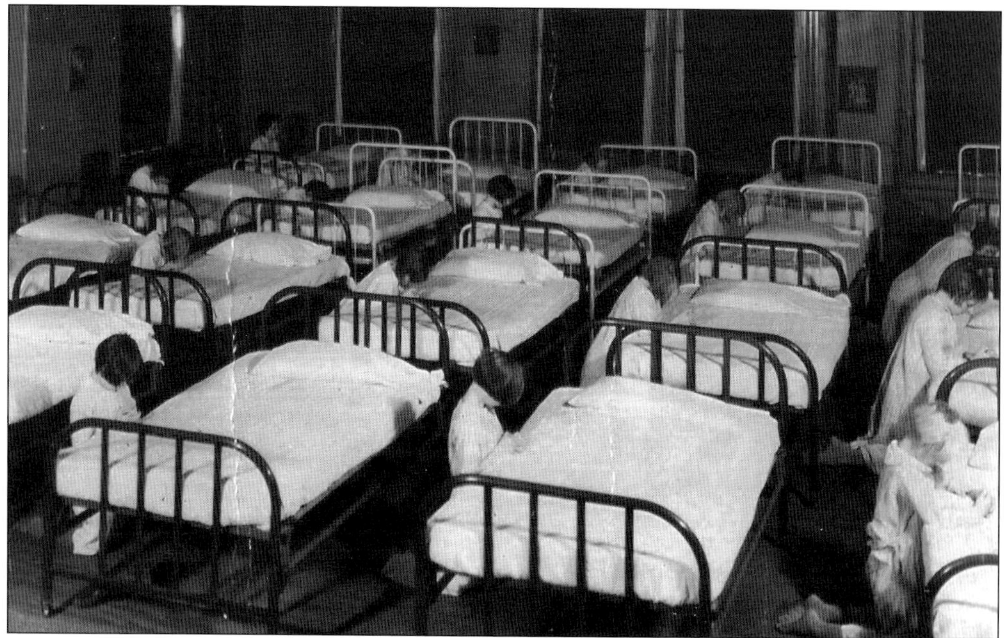

Prayer at bedtime was a nightly ritual instilled in the children who lived at the orphan's home, as seen here in the dormitory for girls. (Courtesy of Glade Run Lutheran Services.)

A Christmas appeal was sent to the community and supporters of the Orphan's Home and Farm School showing a group of young boys and girls in the 1940s. The appeal made a plea for funding for a new modern cottage. Funds were being raised to memorialize Dr. C.W. White, who worked long and unselfishly, dedicating years of service to the children. (Courtesy of Glade Run Lutheran Services.)

Glade Run has served thousands who passed through the doors as broken individuals and emerged whole. From the humble beginnings of the Orphan's Home and Farm School, Glade Run's mission and spirit have remained constant throughout the years, offering development and compassion to those in need. (Courtesy of Glade Run Lutheran Services.)

Merchant and philanthropist Jacob Mark Gusky was a successful department store owner in Pittsburgh who became one of the great benefactors of local orphans. Gusky gave to orphans and widows throughout Pittsburgh during his annual Gift Tour. By 1885, he gave away more than 3,000 gifts to needy children. After his untimely death in 1886 at the age of 41, Gusky's widow, Esther, insisted that his charity to orphans should continue. (Courtesy of the Jewish Association on Aging.)

Judge Josiah Cohen and his wife, Carrie, who had no children of their own, became "parents" to the children at the Gusky Orphanage. Judge Cohen was president of the orphanage, and Carrie played the piano for the children's Sabbath service and donated a Victrola and records to the home so the children could listen to music. (Courtesy of the Jewish Association on Aging.)

In 1939, a merger was proposed by the Gusky Hebrew Orphanage and Home of Western Pennsylvania with the Jewish Home for Babies and Children in Pittsburgh. Fundamental differences intervened in that the Gusky Orphanage was supported by charities and children would be placed in foster homes. The Home for Babies provided for children within the facility. The initiative failed. (Courtesy of the Rauh Jewish Archives at the Heinz History Center.)

The Gusky Orphanage opened 1891 and was located on Perrysville Avenue in the North Side of Pittsburgh. With Riverview Park just one block away, the location was chosen for its benefits of the open countryside and clean air. The orphanage was operated by volunteers, staff, and supporters who donated money, clothing, and other needs for the orphaned children. By 1920, the facility could accommodate nearly 100 children. (Courtesy of the Rauh Jewish Archives at the Heinz History Center.)

When orphanages were denominational homes in the late 1800s, there was no place specifically for Jewish orphans in Pittsburgh. To address this need and to memorialize Jacob Gusky's extraordinary compassion for orphaned children, his generous widow, Esther Gusky, founded a Jewish institution serving that cause. Children at the Gusky Orphanage ranged in age from two to 15 years old. All were housed in the residences and educated in public schools. (Courtesy of the Rauh Jewish Archives at the Heinz History Center.)

This image of children in the early 1900s is testimony to Jacob Gusky's impact on the community through his generosity and the hope he inspired among the orphans. His name was perpetuated through the J.M. Gusky Orphanage and Home, and his legacy became a blessing to thousands of needy children and families. Proceeds from the sale of the property in 1943 helped fund the Jewish Family and Children's Service of Pittsburgh. (Courtesy of the Rauh Jewish Archives at the Heinz History Center.)

On April 5, 1832, the Protestant Orphan Asylum of Pittsburgh and Allegheny was founded by the First Presbyterian Church for abandoned, neglected, and orphaned children west of the Alleghenies. By the early 1900s, the institution became known as the Protestant Orphan Home. (Courtesy of Pressley Ridge.)

A second orphanage, known as the Home for the Friendless, was incorporated in 1861 by the Second Presbyterian Church. The name was changed in 1866 to the Pressley House, the street name where the building was located. Serving the same community, the Protestant Orphan Home cared for true orphans, and the Home for the Friendless looked after children who were abused or neglected but who may still have had living parents. (Courtesy of Pressley Ridge.)

The Civil War took a heavy toll on soldiers from Pittsburgh. At one time, it was estimated that the Home for the Friendless cared for more than 500 children of the men who were killed in action. For more than a century, the institution continued to serve populations of children in the Pittsburgh community. (Courtesy of Pressley Ridge.)

By the 1960s, the Protestant Home and the Pressley House merged to become Pressley Ridge School. Though no longer referred to as an orphanage, modern-day Pressley Ridge continues to operate today serving children and families facing difficulties. Its services include foster care and adoption, therapy counseling, and specialized residential programs for children, reaching about 10,000 families each year. (Both, courtesy of Pressley Ridge.)

Before Wilbur Emory McKiernan died in 2012 at the age of 96, he set up a trust within his estate to go to an organization that had played a pivotal role in his life. In 1927, McKiernan and his younger brother Richard were surrendered to the Pittsburgh and Allegheny Home for the Friendless, an orphanage in the North Side of Pittsburgh today known as Pressley Ridge. Wilbur entered the Home for the Friendless in 1925 at the age of nine. A photograph taken shortly before shows Wilbur standing on porch steps (right) behind his mother, Eva Flinn McKiernan (right). Eva divorced her husband and, for unknown reasons, turned her sons over to the orphanage. McKiernan never forgot the care he received as an orphan. He married Juanita Weaver in 1951, and a year later, they began fostering children and became involved in numerous programs dealing with the special needs of children. Throughout their lifetime, it was estimated that they touched more than 1,800 lives of young children. (Courtesy of the McKiernan family.)

In 1859, when the Episcopal Church Home first opened its doors in downtown Pittsburgh, it was one of the first charities, determined to provide for elderly women who had no place to go. Soon, the need to shelter orphans became evident, and the charter was quickly amended. Two years later in 1861, the Episcopal Church Home purchased the Locust Grove Seminary for Girls in Lawrenceville on the corner of Penn Avenue and Fortieth Street. The larger space came just in time to help care for the growing population of Civil War orphans. By 1880, the Episcopal Church Home cared for 66 orphaned children, 7 aging women, and 7 young apprentices. (Courtesy of Canterbury Place.)

The Home for Colored Children was founded in Pittsburgh in 1880 after Rev. James Fulton, a Presbyterian minister, found a young Black girl, barely five years old, roaming the streets alone with no one to care for her. The minister took her to his home for a time and soon began to work with the Women's Christian Association to help to lay the foundation for an orphanage for Black children. The home began operation in a small home in Allegheny City on the North Side of Pittsburgh. What followed was a groundbreaking venture and only the second of its kind in the nation to provide care specifically for Black orphan children who were not accepted at other established orphanages. The census from 1900 showed that 55 children were living in the Home for Colored Children. (Both, courtesy of Three Rivers Youth.)

The Home for Colored Children would grow and move to several locations before establishing on six acres in the area of the city. A photograph from Christmas 1935 shows orphaned children eating their holiday meal together in the dining room of the Home for Colored Children in Pittsburgh. (Courtesy of Three Rivers Youth.)

The Home for Colored Children was founded by a group of women in 1880 and was one of the few organizations serving African American families until after 1900, when institutions led by Blacks expanded, responding to persistent racism. The organization today is known as Three Rivers Youth (TRY) and has continued the mission of preserving and uniting families, addressing homelessness, enhancing educational opportunities, and helping to build life skills for youths at risk. With more than a century of experience, TRY has achieved its mission through programs and services that reach more than 5,500 local youths and families each year. (Both, courtesy of Three Rivers Youth.)

The Pittsburgh Newsboys Home was developed in 1885 as a school located at Fifth and Liberty Avenues. A second building, shown at the corner of Forbes, Shinghiss, and Sixth Avenues, was constructed in 1899 with the addition of a home and an industrial training department. The Pittsburgh Newsboys Home received generous support from the public, the *Pittsburgh Press*, Mary Schenley, and Christopher Magee. (Courtesy of the Pennsylvania Department of Carnegie Library.)

Boys who were too old to be kept in an orphanage found meals and lodging in dormitory-style living on the third floor of the Pittsburgh Newsboys Home. Young males were also taught trades to help them secure work in the printing and machine shop trades, most likely the only training they would receive for future development. For the majority, chances of further school were slim after leaving the institution, as many had no home to return to after they reached the age of 12. In the early 1960s, the Pittsburgh Newsboys Home property was acquired by Duquesne University. (Both, courtesy of the Pennsylvania Department of Carnegie Library.)

In 1884, a desperate woman left a baby outside of a Pittsburgh home occupied by the Sisters of Charity of Seton Hill. The baby did not survive, but a ministry began for unwed mothers, many who could not care for their infants on their own and sought help in secret. The hospital had 60 beds and a waiting list of up to 100 for women who became residents during their pregnancy and after giving birth. In 1891, the Sisters of Charity opened a foundling asylum where infants could be left safely and in secret. In the first four months, 64 babies were abandoned and left as foundlings. These early images show the original building and the Roselia Foundling nurses, infants, and children outside of the home. (Both, courtesy of the Archives of the Sisters of Charity of Seton Hill.)

A photograph from the 1950s shows the newly built Roselia Foundling and Maternity Hospital, dedicated to caring for unmarried mothers and children, as well as caring for foundlings and orphans. The new building had a maternity ward staffed by doctors from Mercy Hospital and eventually had its own medical staff, social workers, and a fully accredited nursing school. When the hospital closed in the late 1960s, the closing was blamed on a changing society, which made unwed motherhood less of a stigma, but in reality, it closed because of the cost of keeping up a building that was too large for the declining number of those who needed the services that were provided. (Courtesy of the Archives of the Sisters of Charity of Seton Hill.)

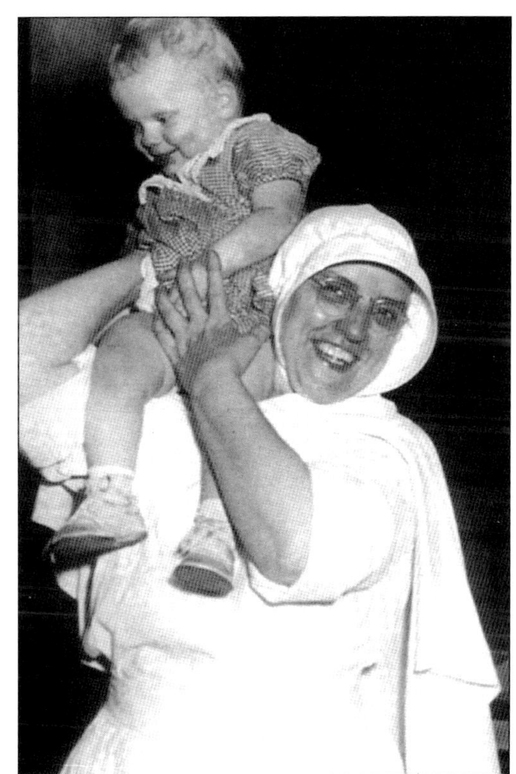

Sr. Mary Kieran Beyer, a dedicated nun who worked with babies until a home was found, is seen with some of the infants and toddlers she cared for at the Roselia Foundling Home. (Both, courtesy of the Archives of the Sisters of Charity of Seton Hill.)

The Pittsburgh Home for the Babies was founded in 1904 by a group of local women and based on a national model of similar organizations operating across the United States at the time. The Pittsburgh Home for Babies was inspired by the philanthropic work of Jane Addams, who received the Nobel Peace Prize in 1931 for her pioneering work as a social worker. The home's original location was 2501 Center Avenue, a residential area of Pittsburgh. In 1918, the home moved to the Von Bonhorst mansion at 317 West Prospect Avenue. The grand property was purchased by board members and other donors. (Courtesy of the Pennsylvania Department of Carnegie Library.)

In the early years of its existence, the Home for Babies was supported by its board of directors who gave, earned, and solicited money to maintain the institution. The board managed the social work as well as the adoptions of the babies. In later years, the home was the beneficiary of several estates, which paid for needed repairs and the hire of qualified and trained professionals. (Both, courtesy of the Pennsylvania Department of Carnegie Library.)

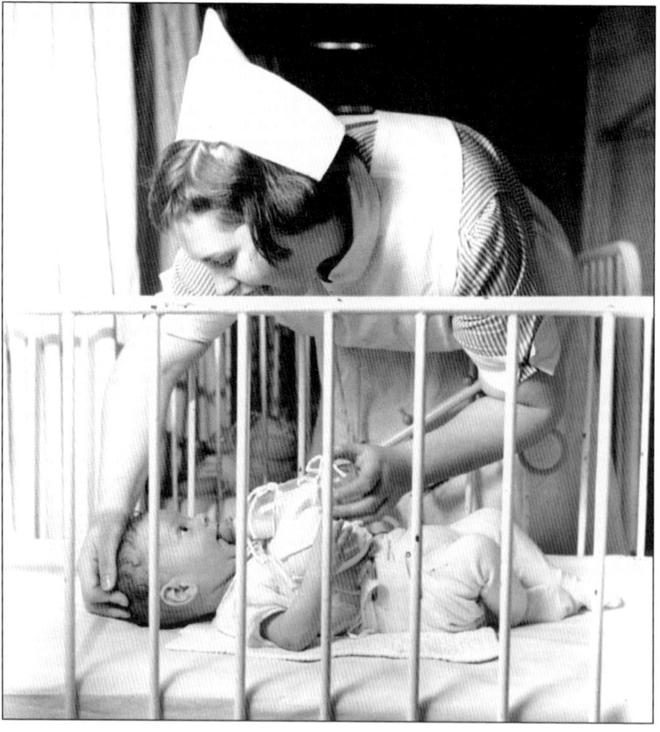

Unlike similar organizations that cared for infants throughout the United States, the Pittsburgh Home for Babies remained open and prospered after World War II. The home was considered a model institution and one of the best run in the country, with a paid staff of nurses, pediatricians, and specialists. The home eventually closed in 1959 due to changes in national policies on caring for dependent infants. These images from the 1950s depict the skilled and loving care given to infants and toddlers by the dedicated nursing staff, who treated the babies as if they were their own. (Both, courtesy of the Pennsylvania Department of Carnegie Library.)

Five

Diocese of Pittsburgh Orphanages

There was a strong Catholic presence in the Pittsburgh area throughout most of the 19th and 20th centuries. As a result of concern for the welfare of orphans and homeless children, there were several orphanages established by the Roman Catholic diocese or Catholic beneficial societies. The Roman Catholic Diocese of Pittsburgh had not yet been created when the Sisters of St. Joseph in Emmitsburg, Frederick County, Maryland, founded St. Paul's Roman Catholic Orphan Asylum of Pittsburgh in 1838. The first site on Second Avenue cared only for girls, but by 1851, St. Paul's expanded its mission to include orphaned boys. The orphanage had a long history in Pittsburgh until a fire forced St. Paul's to close its doors in 1965, and the children living there were transferred to Holy Family Institute.

In 1872, the Sisters of the Good Shepherd established the Home of the Good Shepherd for orphaned girls and young women, beginning in a house belonging to the Sisters of Mercy on Pride and Bluff Streets. Another Catholic orphanage was St. Michael's (German) Orphan Asylum. Established in 1874 in the South Side of Pittsburgh, this institution provided care for the orphans of St. Michael's Parish. In April 1893, St. Joseph Protectory for Homeless Boys was established as an industrial home where boys were taught the printing trade.

The Capuchin Franciscan Friars opened the Toner Institute in 1899. Originally in Derry Township, Westmoreland County, the institute moved in 1914 to Brookline, where the facility served homeless boys.

Just outside Pittsburgh in Emsworth, the Sisters of the Holy Family of Nazareth created the Holy Family Institute in 1903. Originally supported by the Polish congregations of the Diocese of Pittsburgh, the sisters cared for children of Polish descent.

Eudes Institute was established in 1906 in the Lincoln Avenue section of Pittsburgh's East End as a home for wayward girls and friendless and homeless children. The last Catholic orphanage that opened in Pittsburgh was the St. Raphael Temporary Home. Opened in 1921 at 3715 Penn Avenue in the Lawrenceville section of Pittsburgh, the facility was administered by the Servants of the Sacred Heart.

The Orphan Asylum of the Holy Family began in 1900 when three orphans were brought to a home for the Sisters of Holy Family of Nazareth in the borough of Emsworth along the Ohio River in Allegheny County. The orphaned children had lost their Polish immigrant parents after an accidental fire, and the sisters were given the responsibility of caring for the children. An early photograph shows children playing outside of the original orphanage. In 1931, the name was changed to Holy Family Institute due to a shift from being only an orphanage to becoming a small-group living facility to serve both orphans and other children in need. (Courtesy of Holy Family Institute.)

The Sisters of the Holy Family of Nazareth, who staffed the Holy Family Orphanage as teachers, caregivers, and nurses, show their playful side after a snowfall in the winter of 1929. A group photograph from 1934 shows the Sisters of the Holy Family of Nazareth. (Both, courtesy of Holy Family Institute.)

A photograph taken in 1930 shows the interior of the original chapel at Holy Family Institute. The chapel was a place of worship and daily prayer for those who lived and worked at the Holy Family home. (Courtesy of Holy Family Institute.)

In an image from 1950, Sister Videntia is seen teaching young orphans how to do laundry and fold clothes, practical chores that children were expected to do from a young age. Another photograph shows Sister Zusanna taking care of the little girls in 1940, making sure that everyone has enough to drink. (Both, courtesy of Holy Family Institute.)

Sisters Martha and Merici supervise orphans at the swimming pool on a hot summer day in the 1940s. The orphans at Holy Family looked forward to playing sports and the physical outdoor activities that were a regular part of the day for those living at the orphanage. (Courtesy of Holy Family Institute.)

An image from the 1940s shows a crowded classroom at Holy Family Institute with children sitting close together sharing a desk while a Sister of the Holy Family supervises and teaches a daily lesson. (Courtesy of Holy Family Institute.)

An undated photograph shows some of the orphan children who lived at Holy Family Institute surrounding Sister Antonia with happy smiles. Many children who were raised in orphanages missed the childhood comforts that others took for granted. Being hugged or tucked into bed at night were emotional signs of affection that orphans lacked, but nuns like Sister Antonia offered love and care, often acting as a surrogate parent. (Courtesy of Holy Family Institute.)

Young orphan girls in the chapel at Holy Family Institute are seen saying their prayers in a photograph taken in 1953. (Courtesy of Holy Family Institute.)

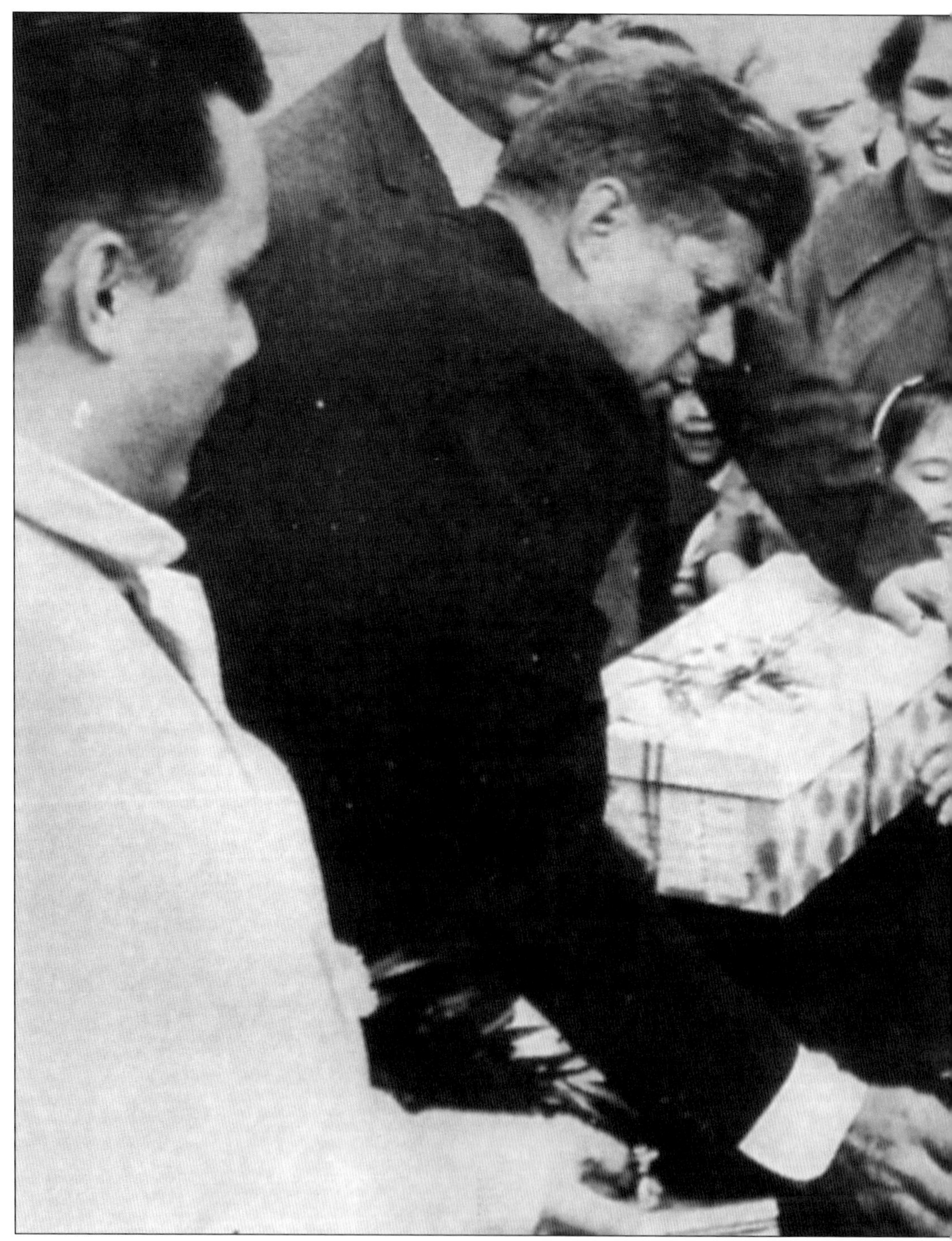

Children of Holy Family Institute had a rare opportunity to meet Pres. John F. Kennedy in 1962 when his motorcade stopped near the orphanage in Emsworth. The children presented the president with a doll for his daughter, Caroline, and later received a letter from Evelyn Lincoln, personal secretary to the president. The letter stated that President Kennedy "was particularly pleased by the friendly gesture and wanted you to know that Caroline was delighted with the cute doll.

The president appreciated the kindness of all who had a part in the presentation of these gifts and asked me to extend every good wish to all of you at Holy Family Institute." The newspaper photographer who took this picture said that President Kennedy was very impressed with the children's good manners and smiles and complimented them as Pittsburgh's finest representatives. (Courtesy of Holy Family Institute.)

St. Anthony's, founded in 1921 by Fr. Boniventure Piscopo, was built on the Hulton Road between Thirteenth and Fifteenth Streets in Oakmont, a suburb of Pittsburgh. St. Anthony's originally ministered to orphans of Italian descent and later catered to children with disabilities. This early photograph shows the original farmhouse that became a home for orphans. (Courtesy of the Archives & Records Center of the Catholic Diocese of Pittsburgh.)

Known as St. Anthony Village, the larger building was erected in 1925 to accommodate more children. The village provided not only a home but also an academic education and faith training for the children in its care. St. Anthony's School for Exceptional Children reveals the size of the complex. The original classroom building is seen here. The larger classrooms and chapel were added in 1959. (Courtesy of the Archives & Records Center of the Catholic Diocese of Pittsburgh.)

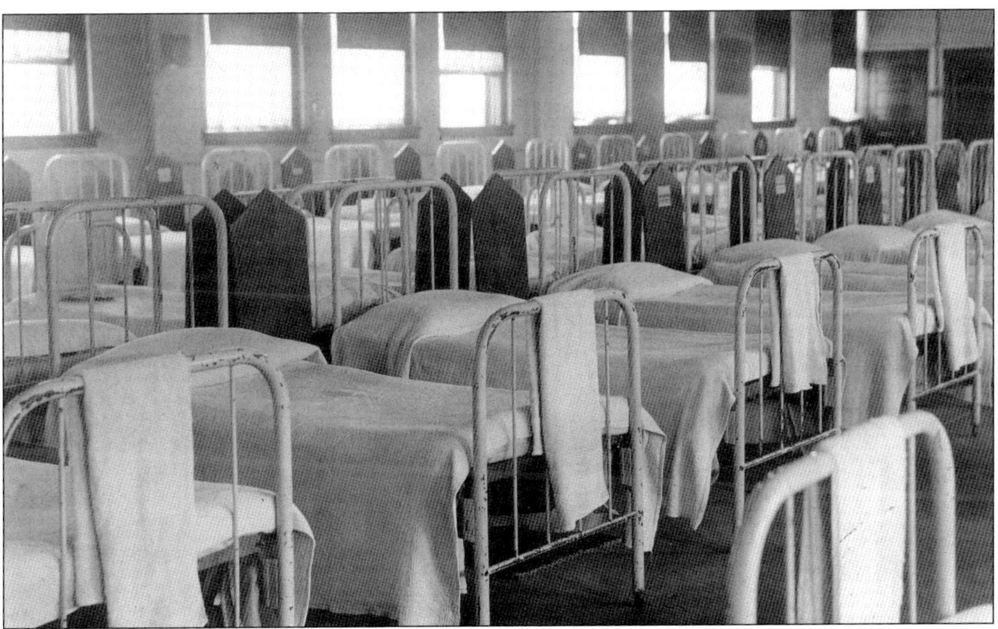

Beds are lined up in rows in the original dormitory, built in 1925. The dormitory was later upgraded to become a new larger room for boys in 1936. (Courtesy of the Archives & Records Center of the Catholic Diocese of Pittsburgh.)

A large group of orphans is seen with two nuns from St. Anthony's and several lay people in the 1920s. All orphans were dressed and groomed alike; the girls had short hair for easier care. (Courtesy of the Archives & Records Center of the Catholic Diocese of Pittsburgh.)

The class of 1929 poses outside with several nuns and priests who were part of the staff and faculty at St. Anthony's. When the school opened, there were 45 students, but the numbers consistently increased, leading to the expansion in 1959. St. Anthony's Village closed in 1953 due to changing times and a significant drop in enrollment and later reopened as St. Anthony's School for Exceptional Children. (Courtesy of the Archives & Records Center of the Catholic Diocese of Pittsburgh.)

Children living at St. Anthony's had plenty of room to play outdoors on the grounds. Daily recess, weekends, and special summertime activities offered welcome recreation and a break from school as seen in this photograph of children at a St. Anthony's picnic held in the 1940s. (Courtesy of the Archives & Records Center of the Catholic Diocese of Pittsburgh.)

Summer picnics were always considered the highlight of the year, as was the treat of eating watermelon. This image from the early 1950s shows residents and staff from St. Anthony's Orphanage in Oakmont. In the back row are nuns who were members of the Apostles of the Sacred Heart, who staffed St. Anthony's during its operation. (Courtesy of the Archives & Records Center of the Catholic Diocese of Pittsburgh.)

Boys and girls from St. Anthony's were often treated to annual outings to amusement parks or special field trips to the Arnold Carnival, as seen in this photograph from 1952. The nearby community of Arnold was approximately 15 miles northeast of Pittsburgh across the Allegheny River from the orphanage, and the children would travel by bus to enjoy a special day out. (Both, courtesy of the Archives & Records Center of the Catholic Diocese of Pittsburgh.)

Children eat in the dining hall at St. Anthony's in the 1940s. By the 1990s, a decline in enrollment occurred when the children were mainstreamed to other schools, and soon after, St. Anthony's Institute closed permanently. (Courtesy of the Archives & Records Center of the Catholic Diocese of Pittsburgh.)

The holidays were a magical time for children from St. Anthony's, who looked forward to receiving Christmas presents from Santa Claus every year, as seen in this photograph taken in 1948. Business owners and members of the local community generously donated to make sure that every child had a gift and felt special. (Courtesy of the Archives & Records Center of the Catholic Diocese of Pittsburgh.)

Orphan children from St. Paul's can be seen on the lawn in front of the orphanage, lined in formation for some type of ceremony as spectators watch in the early 1920s. This location was St. Paul's third site, located on a plateau known as Idlewood between the neighborhoods of Crafton and Carnegie in Pittsburgh. In 1919, the number of children residing there reached a peak of 1,200. (Courtesy of the Archives & Records Center of the Catholic Diocese of Pittsburgh.)

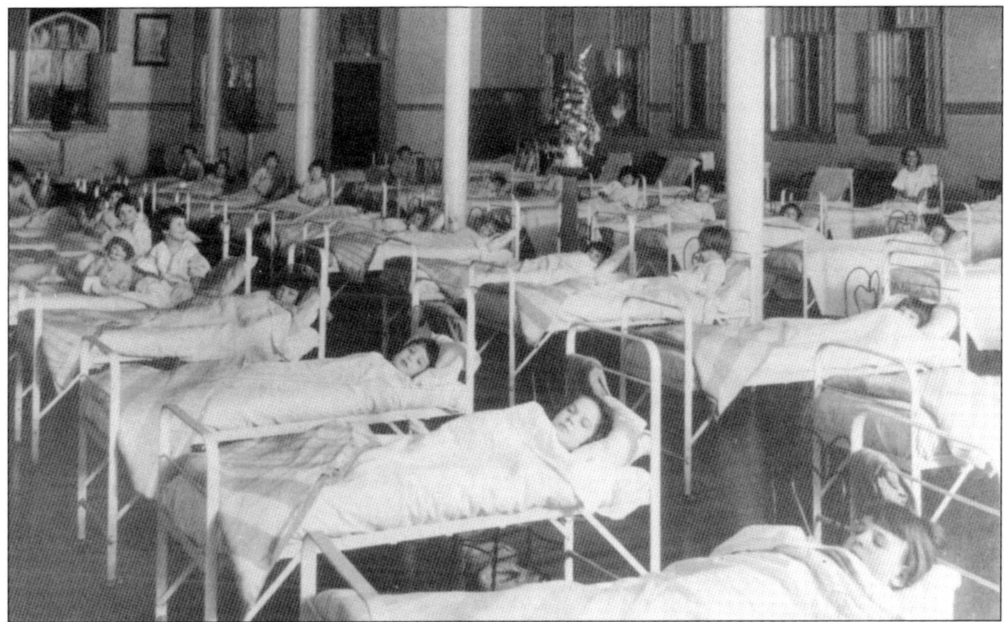

In addition to acquiring more land, other improvements were steadily made at St. Paul's, including a chapel wing in 1907, a hospital unit in 1911, a separate school building in 1920, a new maintenance building in 1924, and new dormitories in the late 1920s. Girls who lived at St. Paul's in 1936 are seen in the dormitory at bedtime. (Courtesy of the Archives & Records Center of the Catholic Diocese of Pittsburgh.)

Children enjoy the swimming pool in the new recreation center at Bishop O'Connor Hall, which was dedicated in 1956—a welcome addition to St. Paul's. (Courtesy of the Archives & Records Center of the Catholic Diocese of Pittsburgh.)

From an early age, the children at St. Paul's were taught to say grace before each meal. A large Christmas tree on display in the dining room gives the orphanage the semblance of a home during the holiday season. (Courtesy of the Archives & Records Center of the Catholic Diocese of Pittsburgh.)

Boys from St. Paul's Orphanage had the opportunity to participate in sports and play for the school team. Football players wearing their uniforms pose for a photograph on the campus of the orphanage in the early 1940s. (Courtesy of the Archives & Records Center of the Catholic Diocese of Pittsburgh.)

St. Paul's orphan children were guests on the television show *Musical Sketchpad*, pictured with host Marty Wolfson, a local pioneer in children's programming. Children of the first TV generation were exposed to art and learning on the program, which aired in the 1950s on WDTV (later KDKA). The host would draw pictures while playing music and telling stories to engage the young audience. (Courtesy of the Archives & Records Center of the Catholic Diocese of Pittsburgh.)

Children from St. Paul's greet Santa Claus at the nearby Pennsylvania Air National Guard base. The annual Christmas event took place in the 1950s and was always a highlight to the boys and girls who would greet Santa on the runway as he arrived from an airplane. (Courtesy of the Archives & Records Center of the Catholic Diocese of Pittsburgh.)

Seen here is the dedication plate on the newly built Bishop O'Connor Hall at St. Paul's Orphanage in 1956. (Courtesy of the Archives & Records Center of the Catholic Diocese of Pittsburgh.)

An aerial view of St. Paul's Orphanage in the 1950s shows the large campus grounds and facilities that included a social hall, chapel, hospital, school, and recreational building. (Courtesy of the Archives & Records Center of the Catholic Diocese of Pittsburgh.)

Six

Individuals Who Left Imprints

Being called a home kid, one who was raised in an orphanage, became a branding. Often, that branding defined the orphans more so than any genetic traits or ethnicity. The label became a state of mind that could never be forgotten. Each individual's personal story is a poignant reminder of a way of life in the years after the Civil War and leading up to World War I, the 1918 influenza pandemic, and the Great Depression. That time is equally important as a piece of Pittsburgh's socioeconomic history that has all but vanished from official documents and record books. Today, more than a century later and too far removed from that era, it is difficult for modern society to comprehend.

Census records show that in the early 1900s, orphanages in the United States housed more than 100,000 children—thousands of those orphans living in Pittsburgh. In most orphanages, everything was communal, and privacy was nonexistent. Children slept in overcrowded dormitories, waited in lines to use a lavatory, and lost their individuality to the uniform appearance of an orphan.

A valuable benefit of being a home kid was developing a sense of resilience and perseverance. Through shared circumstances at an early age, children learned empathy and understanding that served them well as adults. The ability to overcome adversity was seen in orphans like Joseph Harrier, who began his life at the Home for the Friendless, and Jim Sleigh, who not only began his life at the Concordia Orphans Home but has come full circle and now lives on the same property in Concordia's senior living community. Margaret Schall was raised in the Odd Fellows Home for Orphans, as were the Kennedy siblings, Ron Todd, and Fred Peterson. Estranged from his family, Nelson Buys lived and worked on a farm in rural Pennsylvania—preparing him well to become a successful business owner. Christine Zagal D'Alessandro spent her childhood at St. Paul's Orphanage, never giving up hope of one day having a family and home of her own. Each of these individuals and thousands more unknowns left lasting imprints as a testimony to their remarkable lives that overcame hardships.

By the time Frederick Raymond Peterson (left) was born in 1921, his mother had been married three times. Her struggles began after her first husband died young, and later, her second marriage failed. Her third husband was the father of her two sons, but their marriage was brief when the young mother passed away a few years later. Frederick L. Peterson was left a widower and made the difficult decision to place his young boys in the Odd Fellows Home for Orphans in Pittsburgh. The early photograph below shows Fred with a family member who visited him while he was living at the orphanage in the 1930s. (Both, courtesy of Larry Peterson.)

Young Fred Peterson is pictured in his baseball uniform playing on the team for the Odd Fellows Home for Orphans in the 1930s. Though the young boys and girls lacked the influence and guidance and involvement of parents while living in the orphanage, they were given opportunities to participate in sports and other extracurricular activities that taught skills and kept them occupied as young children. (Courtesy of Larry Peterson.)

Fred Peterson (third row, first from left) stands with his graduation class from John Morrow School in 1938. John Morrow School was located on Davis Avenue, only a block away and a short walk from the Odd Fellows Home for Orphans on Fleming Avenue. All of the orphans who lived at the Odd Fellows Home attended the John Morrow School. (Courtesy of Larry Peterson.)

Fred Peterson joined the Navy after high school and returned to visit orphans at the Odd Fellows Home, as seen in this photograph taken while on leave. He was assigned to the USS *Northampton* in 1941 at the time of the attack on Pearl Harbor, but a fortuitous delay for refueling kept the ship at sea until December 8, sparing his life from the horrendous casualties. (Both, courtesy of Larry Peterson.)

Irene Mary Petro (right) was born in 1925 in Kentucky and later moved to Pittsburgh after her mother died. She spent her childhood and teenage years living at St. Paul's Orphanage with her two sisters. Despite having a family and relatives who would often visit and remain involved in her life, Irene was considered an orphan due to the loss of one parent. In many instances, children were relinquished to orphanages when a family could no longer care for them. Often, the hope was that this would be a temporary placement, but most children stayed until graduating out of the system at the age of 18. (Courtesy of Larry Peterson.)

A photograph shows some members of the Petro family and relatives during a visit to St. Paul's Orphanage, located in the Pittsburgh neighborhood of Crafton. The three Petro sisters lived at St. Paul's from the time they were young girls throughout their teenage years. (Courtesy of Larry Peterson.)

Fred Peterson and Irene Petro met through their siblings and quickly became a couple, discovering their shared experience of being raised in an orphanage. Fred lived at the Odd Fellows Orphanage, while Irene grew up at St. Paul's Orphanage, both in Pittsburgh, during the 1930s. After graduation, they moved to New Jersey, married in 1946, and raised a family that included four children, grandchildren, and great-grandchildren. (Courtesy of Larry Peterson.)

Shortly after the death of his wife in 1943, Robert Kennedy placed his five children in the Odd Fellows Home for Orphans because he was unable to care for them on his own. Though the siblings stayed together and had each other for comfort and support, the absence of their parents left lasting impressions that shaped their lives. Pictured from left to right are (first row) Rhoda, Rebecca, and Robert Blair Jr; (second row) Robert Kennedy Sr., Morna, and Patricia. (Courtesy of Rebecca Kennedy McVicker.)

Madelyn Ruth Hall Kennedy was only 29 in 1943 when she died days after being badly burned in a house fire sparked by spilled kerosene. She left five children motherless, ages 8 to 18 months, the youngest still in a crib, and her husband, Robert Kennedy, who was ill equipped to care for his children. He took them to an orphanage, where they would live, eat, and sleep amidst a multitude of other children for the rest of their childhood and as teenagers. (Courtesy of Rebecca Kennedy McVicker.)

Robert Kennedy joined the Navy after becoming a widower. When he would visit his children at the orphanage, they would often spend time playing outdoors and searching the lawn for four-leaf clovers. If one was found, the father would reward his children with a nickel, enough for a popsicle from the nearby grocery store. Sometimes, the children would receive candy from their father but later turn it over to staff at the orphanage. (Courtesy of Rebecca Kennedy McVicker.)

The Kennedy children became orphans of circumstance when their mother died and their father, Robert Kennedy, was unable to cope with raising a family on his own. His visits to the orphanage were seldom, and the siblings have sad memories of being promised that he would see them, yet he would never show up. Many times, the Kennedy children would sit for hours on the steps of the orphanage waiting with a false sense of hope at every car that passed, only to be let down by their father's unreliability. The painful memories of disappointment and abandonment stayed with the Kennedys throughout their lives except for the love they received from Odd Fellows superintendents Charles and Ruth Kress. The couple took a special interest in the children and became like grandparents, postponing their retirement until the youngest Kennedy graduated and left the orphanage. (Both, courtesy of Rebecca Kennedy McVicker.)

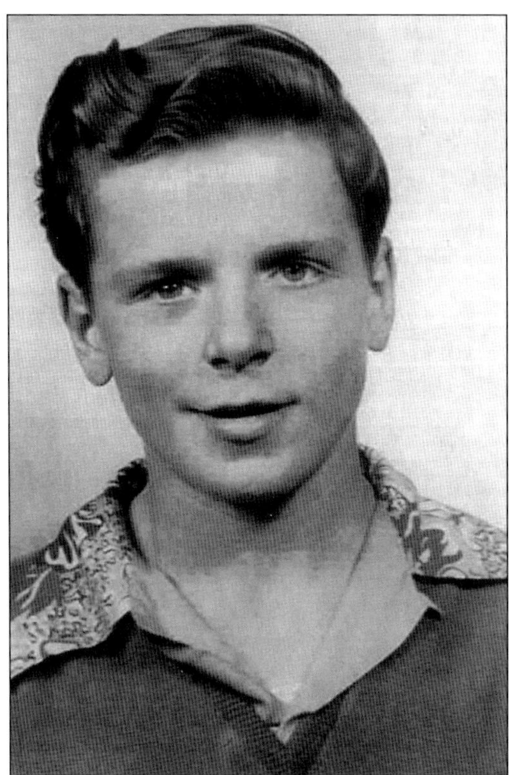

Ronald Todd was placed in a home for infants in 1936, unaware he was the illegitimate son of his young mother and an older father who was married to another woman. As a toddler, he was transferred to the Odd Fellows Home for Orphans, where he recalls the ritual of children lining up to be looked over by families for adoption. He felt lasting rejection from never being selected. (Courtesy of Ron Todd.)

Ron Todd attended elementary school with outside children, yet the stigma of being an orphan followed him, as he was shunned and looked down upon. Often, when home kids were afflicted with tuberculosis or infected with outbreaks of lice, they were pitied by some and mocked by others. Feeling different and alone, this rejection played a major role in the direction his life would take. (Courtesy of Ron Todd.)

At 18, Ronald Todd joined the Navy after the orphanage, and he served active duty on the aircraft carrier USS *Coral Sea* until 1959. In the mid-1960s, Todd moved to California and was hired by 3M in marketing when the company was developing a new product of a playback machine for background music. Todd advanced with 3M, earning numerous marketing awards, and was named Salesman of the Year six times, competing with hundreds of salesmen across the United States. He became Southern California district supervisor in 1968 and was later promoted to district manager for Santa Barbara, Las Vegas, and Hawaii. Coming from humble beginnings, Ron Todd saw the success he experienced as a true blessing. (Courtesy of Ron Todd.)

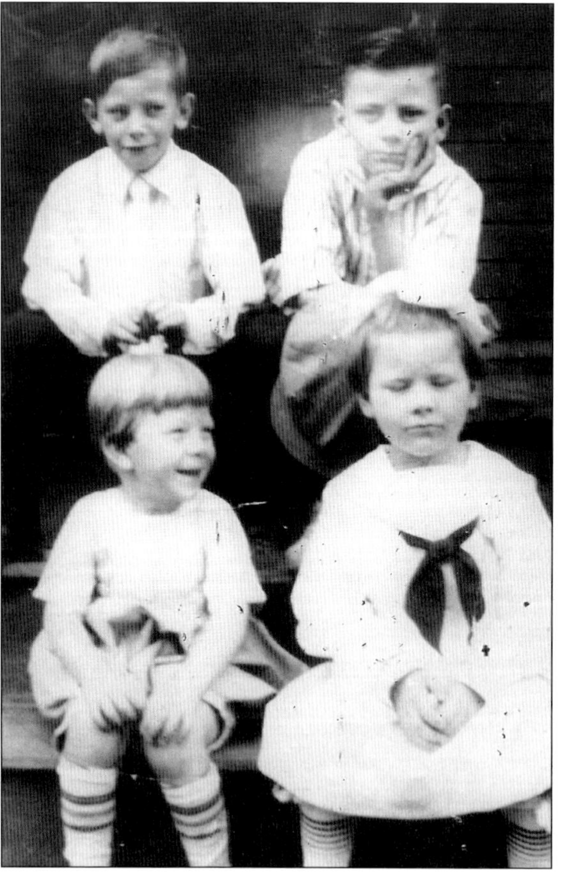

Nelson Buys, pictured above as a toddler in the center of the back row being held on a woman's lap, is seen in an early photograph of the Buys family with relatives taken in the early 1920s. One of the only images of his parents shows Nelson's father, James, sitting in the second row, far left, with his wife, Ethel, directly behind him. Pictured at left, Nelson sits beside his sister, Olive, with his older brothers Jim (left) and Bill (right) behind them. Not long after these photographs were taken, the Buys home in Franklin, Pennsylvania, was destroyed by fire, leaving the family destitute. Nelson and his two older brothers were abandoned and left on their own as orphans, even though their parents survived and relocated. Young Nelson found work on a farm and a family to take him in. His parents never returned for him. (Both, courtesy of Joanne Meade.)

Nelson Buys lived with the McCalmont family, who took him in when he was left orphaned, in the rural community of Sugar Creek, less than five miles from Franklin, where his family had lived. Young Nelson, standing in the first row at far right, is seen in this image with the McCalmonts on their farm in the early 1930s. Mary McCalmont, standing behind Nelson on the far right, was like a surrogate sister to him. (Courtesy of Joanne Meade.)

When asked about his childhood, Nelson Buys described it as a grand adventure, never dwelling on the negative that he was left on his own. He had no bitterness or anger and accepted that his parents did the best they could. In a photograph from Franklin Elementary School, Nelson (top row, fifth from left) adjusted well with other students and never considered himself abandoned or orphaned. (Courtesy of Joanne Meade.)

As a young adult, Nelson Buys was described by his peers as having a personality blessed with dry wit. He had a strong work ethic that began on the farm and later worked on a golf course, where he took interest in learning about trees. He enrolled in a program at Penn State University, which eventually led him to become the founder and owner of Nelson Buys Tree Service in Baldwin borough of Pittsburgh. (Courtesy of Joanne Meade.)

Nelson Buys married Nancy Kleber in 1950, and together, they were blessed with eight children, eleven grandchildren, and five great-grandchildren. From humble beginnings, Buys was a World War II veteran and became a popular person in the Pittsburgh community. A self-taught champion golfer, he was a longtime member of Rolling Hills Country Club, past president of the Great Lakes Seniors Golf Association, and qualified for the US Senior Open in the 1980s. (Courtesy of Joanne Meade.)

Nelson Buys returned to his roots toward the end of his life and went back to visit the original farmhouse (above) where he lived as a child outside of Franklin. He reunited with Mary McCalmont (below), who always treated Nelson as one of her own younger brothers. After a lifetime of being estranged, he also reconnected with his birth sister, Olive, who was living in California. Meeting his sister when Nelson was 89 years old was like meeting a stranger, as they did not know each other throughout life. His visit with Mary was more heartwarming for Nelson, as he fondly reminisced about his youth, grateful for the time when he was welcomed into a home and became part of the McCalmont family. Nelson Buys lived a full life seeing beauty in everything and with an appreciation for his many blessings. (Both, courtesy of Joanne Meade.)

Jim Sleigh (first row, center) stands with friends at the Evangelical Lutheran Concordia Home for Orphans in the early 1950s. Jim was sent to Concordia with his four siblings, all under the age of 10, in 1941. The orphanage was a fully functioning farm, and the children worked hard to keep everyone on the campus fed. Boys as young as 10 would milk 15 cows, gather eggs from 500 chickens, and slop 50 hogs before attending classes each day in a one-room schoolhouse on the grounds. Young girls worked inside, cleaning, cooking, and canning. The orphan children developed a strong work ethic at a young age. They were treated well and cared for at Concordia, but the stigma of being an orphan left a lasting impression on Jim as he remembered being treated differently than kids who had a family. (Courtesy of Concordia Lutheran Ministries.)

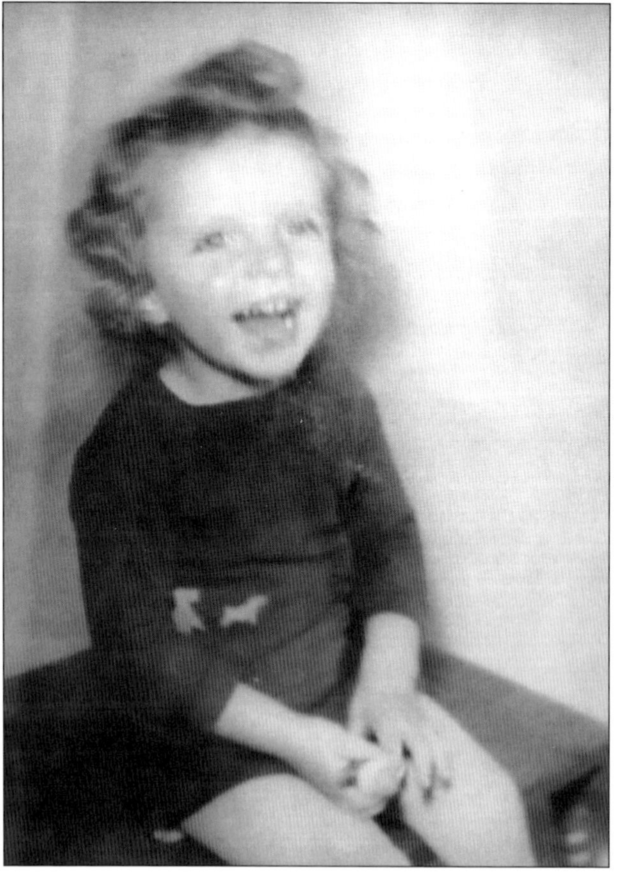

Jim Sleigh stayed at Concordia until he finished high school and joined the Army. Following six years of active duty and reserve, he got a job at Armco Steel (now AK Steel), where he worked for 37 years. He and his wife, Andrea, had five children and seven grandchildren. After living for decades in the home they built in Butler, Pennsylvania, Jim and Andrea decided it was time to downsize and move somewhere they could manage easier. Jim came full circle as he returned to his roots and the couple became residents at Concordia's Haven Retirement Community. Never forgetting his humble beginnings and making the most of his life and the blessings he was given, Jim Sleigh's life advice to others was "Stay within the Lord and give back to others when you can." (Both, courtesy of Concordia Lutheran Ministries.)

Business Men Treat Orphans To Circus

Orphans from North Side were the guests of North Side business men yesterday for a "day at the circus." Jack and Joe Harrier, brothers, are pictured above with Lee Powell, the "Lone Ranger" of the movies, who stars in the Wallace Brothers circus. Matinee and evening performances will be held today at the Farmers Market.

Joseph Harrier entered the Home for the Friendless in 1942 when he was nearly 14 years old. Before that, he and his four siblings moved in and out of state care facilities because their mother was unable to care for her children due to a series of many difficult circumstances in her life. Adapting to constant instability and the stigma of becoming orphans was an overwhelming burden for the young Harrier children to handle. A newspaper clipping shows Joe with his brother Jack and actor Lee Powell, who played the Lone Ranger on television, during a charitable outing to the circus that was funded by local Pittsburgh businessmen. (Courtesy of Joyce Griffin.)

While living at the Home for the Friendless, Joseph Harrier was a bright young man who took art and music classes and became skilled in painting and drawing. He was quick to make friends with his jovial, easy-going personality. Spending time fishing with his friends quickly became a favorite pastime, and many days were spent casting their rods to catch some fish. In the photograph at left, Harrier proudly displays his prized catch of the day. Below, he is second from the left with his fishing buddies from the orphanage. (Both, courtesy of Joyce Griffin.)

A very important aspect of Joseph Harrier's life was his faith in God. As he became an adult, his life changed when he met and married Mary Louise Stahl and had a family of his own, which included three children: Joseph Jr., Bruce, and Joyce. The Harriers found a good church and taught their children to know and serve God. Joseph Harrier's children witnessed his ritual of reading the Bible, and he led by example, sharing his knowledge of the gospels as he grew in his faith and love for Christ. There was always a lot of love, laughter, and forgiveness in the Harrier home, and God was the center of their lives, providing the stability that Joseph never had as a child. (Courtesy of Joyce Griffin.)

Joseph Harrier began working at a young age, holding many jobs in his life, including a stint with Hanover Shoes in Pittsburgh. He also worked at a gas station, delivered newspapers, and worked for McDonald's, sometimes holding three jobs at a time to provide for his family. In 1969, he took a job working for General Motors (GM) and moved his family to Detroit. He went to Macomb Community College in Warren, Michigan, and received several certifications for his position with GM, where he continued to work for 30 years before retiring. A proud career milestone for Joe, pictured with his supervisor, was when he won the Suggestion Award after presenting an idea that GM implemented in the company. (Courtesy of Joyce Griffin.)

Joseph Harrier met Mary Louise Stahl when he was 26, and they married on New Year's Day in 1955. They were blessed with three children and provided a loving home with the stability and security that had been sorely lacking in Joe's life as a child. With God at the center of their lives and an emphasis on the importance of faith, their marriage set an example and left a legacy for their family. (Courtesy of Joyce Griffin.)

Joseph Harrier was proud of his family and set an example as a caring father. An early family photograph from 1970 shows children Bruce (first row, left), Joyce (right), Mary Lou and Joseph, and oldest son Joe (standing behind his parents). The later photograph shows the adult Harrier children (from left to right) Joyce, Bruce, and Joe with their parents on their 50th anniversary. (Both, courtesy of Joyce Griffin.)

Joseph loved Mary Lou deeply until the day he died, and their love, life, and marriage of 62 years made a lasting impact on their children that was honored and cherished. The affection of them embracing, kissing, and telling each other how much they loved each other, even into old age, was a testimony that they were lifelong sweethearts. Pictured are Mary Lou and Joseph celebrating their 50th wedding anniversary in 2005. (Courtesy of Joyce Griffin.)

The earliest memory Christine "Chris" Zagal had from her childhood life was the day her mother left her at St. Paul's Orphanage. Only a toddler, Chris remembered crying uncontrollably while clinging to her mother. Court records showed that Chris's parents, Edward and Margaret Zagal, had been previously evicted from their home and turned to the juvenile court system for assistance. Edward struggled as an alcoholic, and Margaret was declared unfit to care for her children. A state social worker saw the family's poor living conditions and the lack of food and threatened to remove the children from their home. In 1957, three-year-old Christine and 11-year-old Barbara were placed at St. Paul's Orphan's Asylum. For the next eight years, until she was eligible for foster care, the institutional setting of St. Paul's would be the only home young Christine would ever know. (Right, courtesy of the D'Alessandro family; below, courtesy of the Archives & Records Center of the Catholic Diocese of Pittsburgh.)

When Christine Zagal reached the age of 11, she left St. Paul's Orphanage and was placed with a foster family who, unfortunately, mistreated her during the years that she lived in their home. In a twist of fate during that time, Chris was hospitalized after an accident when she met a young friend, Debbie Davis, and her family, who offered a sense of hope. The family began a loving relationship with Chris and accepted her as one of their own. During the hardest times of her life, Chris felt love and acceptance from Marie Davis, who offered motherly love, compassion, and understanding. Chris is seen in this photograph getting ready on her wedding day with Mrs. Davis at her side. A later photograph shows Chris (left) with sisters Donna Davis Walters (center) and Debbie Davis Perkins (right), who kept a lifelong friendship. (Both, courtesy of the D'Alessandro family.)

Christine Zagal set herself on a new path when she met and later married Dale D'Alessandro, a man of strong character who put family first before his own needs and taught Chris the meaning of true and unconditional love. Together, they built a wonderful life and the family that Chris had always prayed for. The days of longing to have a home were behind her as Chris received a spiritual gift: the realization of her many blessings in life. (Courtesy of the D'Alessandro family.)

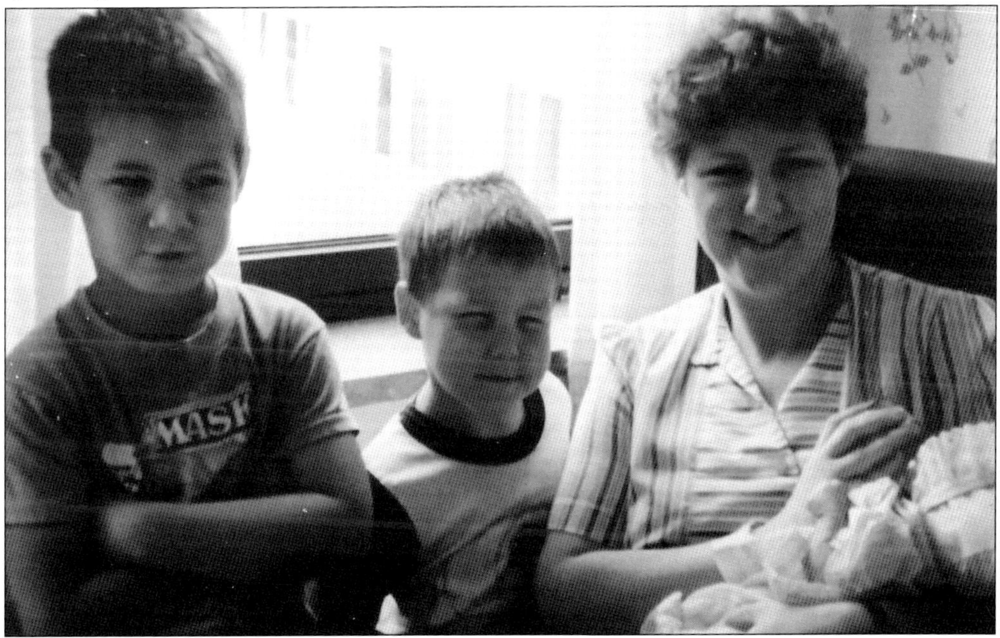

Despite the absence of a true home and family, Chris D'Alessandro became a loving mother to two sons and a daughter. She is pictured with Nicholas (left), Joseph (center), and infant Lindsay. Chris became naturally giving of the motherly love that she never received as a child and learned to create a home that was filled with a sense of appreciation and joy. (Courtesy of the D'Alessandro family.)

As an adult, Chris D'Alessandro lived life to the fullest. Pictured with her dog, Pluto, she was a lover of animals and became an avid bike rider, going on rides several times per week. Influenced by her humble beginnings in an orphanage, Chris became a volunteer advocate for CASA (Court Appointed Special Advocate) for Kids, striving to make a life-changing difference for children who have experienced abuse or neglect. (Courtesy of the D'Alessandro family.)

For 38 years, Christine and Dale D'Alessandro raised their loving family in their beautiful home, the first and only home Chris ever knew. On January 28, 2020, Christine died in the prime of her life from the ravages of ALS disease. She will be remembered for her huge heart, strong faith, and most of all, her love of family. From humble beginnings at St. Paul's Orphanage, her legacy remains through those who loved her. (Courtesy of the D'Alessandro family.)

Bertram Sylvester Schall, the youngest of 10 children of Nicholas and Elizabeth Schall, was born in 1878 in the rural town of Vandergrift, Pennsylvania. At an early age, he went to work in the steel mills, and he married Sarah Emeline Metzler in his early 30s. The young couple is seen outside their home on Kopple Hill near Vandergrift (above) and, below, posing for a portrait with their first three children: Leone (left), Mary (right), and infant George held on his mother's lap. Within a few years after the family portrait was taken, the Schalls had two more daughters, Margaret and Laura Jane, who barely knew their father, Bertram, due to his early death on April 10, 1920, at the age of 42. (Both, courtesy of the Schall family.)

Bertram Sylvester Schall, pictured with his son, George, in 1914, was a member of the Mineral Point Odd Fellows Lodge in Armstrong County, Pennsylvania. The Independent Order of Odd Fellows was one of the largest fraternal orders in the United States in the early 1900s. The IOOF's mission was to assist widows and orphans if misfortune should arise to a member. (Courtesy of the Schall family.)

Sarah Metzler Schall became a widow with five children at the age of 32. The dire circumstances she faced without her husband left her terrified as she wondered how she would provide for her children. That question was answered by the benefits offered by the Odd Fellows Home for Widows and Orphans. (Courtesy of the Schall family.)

This is an early photograph of the Schall children with their mother, Sarah, and their maternal grandparents in 1920 near Vandergrift, Pennsylvania. Missing from the photograph is Sarah's husband, Bertram, who left her a widow with five children at the age of 32. A few months later, on August 4, 1920, the three youngest Schalls, George, Margaret, and Jane, would be relinquished to the first Odd Fellows Home for Orphans in Ben Avon. (Courtesy of the Schall family.)

A later photograph of Sarah Schall with her five children gives the pretense of a family, maybe at one time serving as a hopeful illusion. By definition, there was no family as they never lived together in the traditional sense. The three younger children—George, age six; Margaret, age four; and Jane, age three—were forsaken to the orphanage in 1920 because their mother could not adequately care for them. (Courtesy of the Schall family.)

The Schall children would sometimes reunite with their two older sisters who lived with their mother on rare visits back to their home in Vandergrift, 30 miles northeast of the Odd Fellows Home in Pittsburgh. Because they could take care of themselves and help their mother with household chores, the sisters, Leone and Mary, remained with their mother. The reunions were always a sad time for George, Margaret, and Jane, who lived at the Odd Fellows year-round and could not understand why they could not live with their mother and their siblings instead of living in the orphanage. (Both, courtesy of the Schall family.)

Three months after their father's death in 1920, siblings Margaret (left), George, and Jane Schall (right) were placed in the Odd Fellows Home for Widows and Orphans, where they remained for over a decade from the time they were toddlers until they graduated from high school. Scared and bewildered, the Schall children found themselves in a strange place with nothing familiar but each other. (Courtesy of the Schall family.)

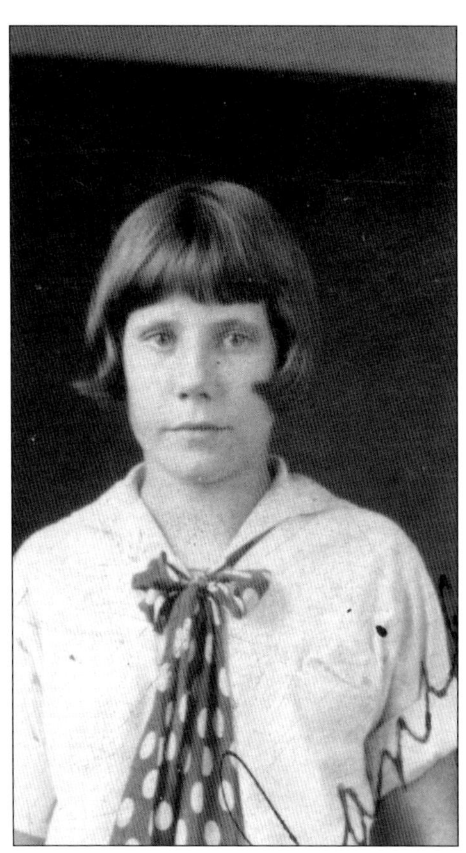

Laura "Jane" Schall entered the Odd Fellows Home for Orphans as a toddler in the early 1920s and lived there during her school years, when she attended nearby John Morrow Elementary School. Jane seldom saw her mother, except for holidays, and often plotted to run away back home only to have those plans defeated at every attempt. (Both, courtesy of the Schall family.)

Margaret Schall, affectionately known as "Tootsie," grew from a child to a young woman at the Odd Fellows Home for Orphans and is seen in this image standing outside the building. The photograph below shows Tootsie (right) as a teenager with her friend, both labeled as home kids. According to records, Margaret graduated from the Odd Fellows Home and was released to her mother on September 1, 1933, after living in the institutional setting for more than 13 years. (Both, courtesy of the Schall family.)

Sisters Margaret and Jane Schall remained close after they left the Odd Fellows Home for Orphans and began their lives as adults in Pittsburgh. Jane married Stanley Krusniewski, seen here on their wedding day in a photograph from the 1930s with Margaret (left) by her side as her witness. The other image shows Margaret as an adult; it was taken several years after she left the orphanage. (Both, courtesy of the Schall family.)

With skills learned in the orphanage, Margaret Schall entered the workforce and became a talented seamstress and, soon after, met and married Henry Belleno. Together, they endured the Great Depression and World War II and had two daughters, followed by a dozen grandchildren and, later, so many great-grandchildren that it became a challenge to keep track of birthdays and ages. Their long-standing marriage weathered many storms and became a relationship that set the ultimate example of perseverance and commitment. Margaret Schall and Henry are pictured in the early 1950s at Niagara Falls, New York, one of their favorite places to visit. (Courtesy of the Schall family.)

Thousands of children who were raised in the Odd Fellows Home and other orphanages adopted the lifelong label of home kid, as seen in this page from a scrapbook. In their own way, they became models of strength and perseverance. Their stories remain an important piece of Pittsburgh's history, along with the institutional settings that gave thousands of orphans a sense of a place to call home. (Courtesy of the Schall family.)

James Caldwell, surrounded by four of his six children, is seen in this 1891 portrait taken in Pittsburgh shortly after his wife, Jessie, died in childbirth. An immigrant who worked in a steel mill, Caldwell did not have family nearby to help, and he turned to an orphanage run by his church to care for his children. His situation was more common than realized and represents the experience of many Pittsburgh families who used orphanages as a temporary measure to deal with childcare. (Courtesy of Jessie Ramey.)

Consistent with our mission to preserve history on a local level, this book was printed in South Carolina on American-made paper and manufactured entirely in the United States. Products carrying the accredited Forest Stewardship Council (FSC) label are printed on 100 percent FSC-certified paper.